Good Things
EMOTIONAL HEALING JOURNAL

COUPLES

A WORKBOOK *FOR* COUPLES
TO CREATE A LOVING, COMMITTED
RELATIONSHIP

Elisabeth Davies, M.C.
Illustrated by **Bryan R. Marshall**

Good Things

EMOTIONAL HEALING JOURNAL for
COUPLES

Elisabeth Davies, M.C.

Illustrations by Bryan R. Marshall

Good Things Emotional Healing Journal for Couples

Trilogy Christian Publishers
A Wholly Owned Subsidary of Trinity Broadcasting Network
2442 Michelle Drive
Tustin, CA 92780

10 9 8 7 6 5 4 3 2 1
Library of Congress Cataloging-in-Publication Data is available.

B-ISBN 978-1-64773-901-0
E-ISBN 978-1-64773-902-7 (ebook)

Acknowledgments

I would like to thank the following:

God, for giving me the gift of writing and the passion to encourage people to live an emotionally healthy lifestyle.

Echo Surina, my editor, for making this workbook professional and giving me helpful feedback regarding format, flow, and better readability. She offered me excellent advice above and beyond what I would expect an editor to do.

Bryan Marshall, my illustrator, for making this workbook visually engaging by creating imagery that enhances the message and content of this workbook. He always amazes me with his talent and creative ideas.

Members of my writer's critique group for reading this workbook and sharing their helpful feedback.

My husband, Stacy, for believing in what I have to offer the world more than I believe in myself. And encouraging me in my pursuit of writing and my passion for helping people emotionally heal.

My clients, who trusted me enough to pour out their hurt and struggles in trying to make their relationship work with a partner they love and for doing the necessary work to have healthier, happier relationships.

Foreword

As you begin to read and use this workbook, remind yourself how important your relationship is. Ask yourself if doing the work suggested in these pages is worth your investment in the future. I hope the answer is yes, for you will now be on your way to success. Relationships can last a lifetime when two people stay focused on the solutions rather than getting bogged down with the problems.

As a couple's counselor, I know the challenges that arise in helping couples navigate their relationship issues toward a positive outcome. I have seen both success and failure. The word "effort" stands out, as it is one of the ingredients necessary for positive results. The rewards are great when it works; it is quite disappointing when it doesn't.

In my practice, I often give homework to couples to assist them in adopting new behaviors to replace their old ways of doing things. Handouts, questionnaires, and articles or books are often suggested. The sad part is that the effort the couples put forth is sometimes poor. Most people want a quick fix to an already long-term dysfunctional relationship, and they simply don't want to do the work.

Here is the good news: a workbook that Elisabeth Davies has written can help make the work easier and more understandable. This workbook is only one of the ways her credentials support her knowledge and expertise.

This workbook may even make the difference between seeing a lawyer, saying new marriage vows, or staying in love forever. The topics Elisabeth covers are right on target, and the exercises are perfectly constructed to help the couple stay the course. In chapter fifteen, she states, "One of the tips is to make your marriage a daily priority." This supports the Relationship Maintenance Agreement that I suggest as a daily reminder of the benefits of a long-term relationship.

Communication, romance, friendship, acceptance, intimacy, and passion are a few areas she covers in this workbook. As an experienced counselor, I know from my own practice that these are key elements to being able to go the distance. Remember that all good things require effort and work. Intimate relationships are no different! They need to be worked on every day, not just when trouble rears its ugly head.

Having a workbook to enhance counseling can be your best friend and a way to monitor your progress, keep the focus, and remind yourself how important your union really is.

Elisabeth Davies is giving this gift in the hope that she can help more people give and receive love, increase self-esteem, develop meaningful closeness with other humans, and decrease the divorce rate.

I am happy that some therapists share my desire to see couples achieve the gift of a lifetime together. Connecting with Elisabeth has given me optimism that this endeavor can be carried out.

I wish this resource had been available to me while I was counseling couples for the past fifteen years. Now, it is yours to use. May you all achieve the ideal relationship you hoped for when you first fell in love.

—Barbara J. Peters,
Licensed Professional Counselor, Relationship Coach,
and Author of *The Gift of a Lifetime*,
Building a Marriage That Lasts: He Said She Said I Said,
7 Keys to Relationship Success, and *Never Too Old for Romance*.

How to Get the Most Out of *Good Things Emotional Healing Journal for Couples*

Good Things Emotional Healing Journal for Couples is an interactive workbook for you to do with your partner, whether you are dating, engaged, or married. The strategies, exercises, and writing prompts in this workbook are designed to help you build a strong foundation of commitment, love, respect, trust, and communication as well as bolster closeness and deepen connection in your relationship. This workbook offers a couple's relationship quiz that will identify your strengths and weaknesses as a couple, along with "love tips" at the end of each chapter to enhance your proficiency as a partner so that you can create a fulfilling, long-lasting relationship together.

As a professional counselor, I have supported thousands of couples in building healthier, more satisfying relationships by using the strategies in this workbook. You will read many of their personal stories in the following chapters. Their names and identifying information have been changed to protect confidentiality. Each couple's unique dynamic will demonstrate how implementing specific skills helped them create a better relationship.

I have been with my one and only husband for more than thirty years. Several years into our marriage, I bought a blank journal and invited him to write down his wants and needs. I reciprocated by writing down my needs and desires for our relationship as well. Not only did I learn new desires of his, but he became more aware of my needs in our marriage. We have continued to write in our couple's journal and share our desires for our marriage through the years. This practice has been a great tool in keeping us close and helping us enjoy being together. Each entry is dated so I can re-read entries from years ago, identify different stages we went through, and appreciate our progress.

My hope is that *Good Things Emotional Healing Journal for Couples* will empower you to practice new skills and develop habits that enhance your intimacy and partnership, making your relationship the best one you have experienced.

Take several minutes each week with your partner to read and write in *Good Things Emotional Healing Journal for Couples*. Read each other's desires, needs, and comments. This should spark conversations that deepen your communication. There are several blank pages for journaling at the end of this workbook. Write, draw, insert pictures, or jot down your own questions to personalize this workbook for you and your partner.

If you prefer verbally communicating your needs and desires to your partner rather than journaling, you can do that. This workbook offers numerous questions that allow you to get to know your partner better and learn what they need, so you can build a great relationship together. Feel free to use *Good Things Emotional Healing Journal for Couples* in any way that improves the time you spend together.

Introduction

You Are Created to Be in a Relationship

Human beings do not thrive in isolation. "The [scientific] literature says clearly that although good habits are important — eating right, exercise, not smoking, etc. — none are as important as high self-esteem and the ability to give and receive love and to develop intimacy with other humans."[i]

WHY DO SO MANY RELATIONSHIPS END?

Approximately forty-five percent of Americans marriages end in divorce and an even higher percentage of relationships end before marriage is even contemplated.[ii] Breakups can teach us a lot about ourselves and what kind of partner we are if we take the time to reflect, but it does not guarantee we will be better at our next relationship.

There are many reasons relationships end: poor communication, infidelity, emotional or physical abuse, untreated addiction, financial troubles, geographic distance, or activities such as work or hobbies that take precedence over the relationship. Just because you want your relationship to work does not mean it will. It takes two and it takes skills.

HOW CAN YOU MAKE YOUR RELATIONSHIP WORK?

If you are dedicated to having a lasting, fulfilling relationship, you must establish a strong foundation that will support its growth. This foundation consists of commitment, communication, trust, respect, and love. If there are weaknesses in these areas, you will struggle, and your relationships will likely not last long-term.

Think back on your past relationships and identify which foundational qualities were lacking and caused the relationship to end. Were you committed to making the relationship work? Was your partner committed? Did you trust him/her? Did he/she trust you? Did you respect him/her? Did he/she respect you? Did you talk about problems that arose in the relationship together? Did you love him/her? Did he/she love you?

In addition to having a strong foundation, it is also important for you and your partner to have a sense of autonomy, otherwise you are likely to become dependent on your partner or controlled. A contributing factor to dependency is caused by a lack of self-worth, which leads to struggles with intimacy, which is essential to maintaining closeness and connection. Therefore, you must possess relationship skills and be willing to work on yourself to have a healthy, fulfilling relationship.

Fortunately, all these skills can be learned and mastered if you are willing to put in the time and effort required. *Good Things Emotional Healing Journal for Couples* is designed to help you with just that so you can avoid the emotional pain of ending a relationship with someone you love.

Table of Contents

Acknowledgments v
Foreword vi
How to Get the Most Out of *Good Things Emotional Healing Journal for Couples* . . . viii
Introduction: You Are Created to Be in a Relationship x

Chapter 1: What You Learn about Relationships Growing Up
       Affects the Way You Do Relationships Today 15
Chapter 2: See How You Score on the Couple's Relationship Quiz 23
Chapter 3: Foundations for Having a Healthy Relationship 31
Chapter 4: How Well Do You Communicate? 41
Chapter 5: How Good Are You at Staying in Love? 51
Chapter 6: Committing for Longevity 59
Chapter 7: Building Trust with Your Partner 69
Chapter 8: Are You Respectful in Your Relationship? 81
Chapter 9: Autonomy in Your Relationship. 93
Chapter 10: Romance Enhancers 105
Chapter 11: More Intimacy and Passion 113
Chapter 12: Building A Deep Friendship with Your Partner 123
Chapter 13: Time for Adventure and Fun 131
Chapter 14: Being Happy in Your Relationship. 141
Chapter 15: Making Your Relationship a Priority. 151
Chapter 16: Becoming Less Self-Centered and More Relationship-Centered 159
Chapter 17: Accepting Your Partner 169
Chapter 18: Forgiving Your Partner. 179
Chapter 19: Reflecting on the Relationship You Are Creating 191

Endnotes 196
About the Author. 197

Elisabeth Davies, M.C.

Chapter 1

What You Learn about Relationships Growing Up Affects the Way You Do Relationships Today

Read this chapter with your partner. Take time to discuss your thoughts, feelings, and opinions about what you learned about relationships growing up.

Your first exposure to how a relationship is supposed to be is influenced by the relationship your parents or role models demonstrated for you growing up. Whether your parents got along, fought, divorced, or remarried, or if one of them abandoned you growing up—all of this influenced what you believe about relationships today. You grew up and began dating. The messages about relationships you received in childhood may have played out in your courting relationships. Perhaps you dated someone who had similar dynamics to one of your parents, or you behaved in a similar way you learned from your parents.

CLIENT STORY

Tina was raised in a family where her dad was the primary financial provider, and her mom did most of the care-taking of the children and home. During her counseling appointment, Tina said, "Mom was expected to have dinner ready for dad when he came home from work, and we were her little helpers. Dad was usually really grumpy and we all kind of walked on eggshells to not agitate him."

I asked Tina what her dad taught her about relationships, and one of the things she said was, "Don't make dad mad, because if you do, things are going to go really bad."

I asked Tina, "What are some things your mom taught you about relationships?" One of the things she said was, "A woman's value comes from serving her husband."

I asked Tina if she had ever been in a relationship where she took on the role of serving or was with a partner who she felt she had to walk on eggshells around. She quickly responded, "I feel like unless I am serving my husband

Gary in some way, I don't bring value as a woman to my relationship. Gary says he has to walk on eggshells with me."

Through counseling, Tina was able to see how she was playing out several different dynamics she had observed from her parents. She and Gary were able to create a more fulfilling marriage over two months just by focusing on what each one was doing individually to create the marriage they both wanted.

It is important to take time and reflect on what you observed from watching your parents' relationship and what advice they gave you about relationships, good or bad. By answering the questions below, you will be able to identify if you or your partner have similar dynamics to those you were raised with and if they play out in your current relationship.

COUPLE'S JOURNAL

Answer these questions separately, then share your answers with each other.

1. What did your mom or female role model teach you about relationships when you were growing up? *(Example: Be strong, take care of the house, be independent)*

_____

_____

_____

_____

_____

_____

_____

_____

_____

_____

_____

_____

_____

_____

2. What did your dad or male role model teach you about relationships when you were growing up? *(Example: Be the provider, be the fun dad or disciplinarian)*

_____

_____

_____

_____

_____

_____

_____

_____

_____

_____

_____

_____

3. Did your mom or dad teach you that males or females have a specific role in a relationship? If so, what are the roles they demonstrated to you? *(Example: Females are the decision-makers in the relationship, males manage the finances)*

_____

_____

_____

_____

_____

_____

_____

_____

_____

_____

_____

4. Do either of you see dynamics in your relationship that were in your parents' relationships? If so, what dynamics? *(Example: Raised with a controlling parent; either you are controlling, or your partner is controlling)*

_____

_____

_____

_____

_____

_____

_____

_____

_____

_____

_____

5. What are the qualities you want to have in your relationship to make it healthy and long-lasting? *(Example: Love, commitment, compromise, shared responsibilities)*

_____

_____

_____

_____

_____

_____

_____

_____

_____

_____

_____

_____

RELATIONSHIP HOMEWORK

By doing this exercise with your partner, both of you become clearer on what you both believe a relationship is.

Take turns completing this sentence using the first ten words that come to mind.

Relationships are...

1.

2.

3.

4.

5.

6.

7.

8.

9.

10.

Do you have any of the same answers? Take time to talk to your partner about what he/she believes a relationship consists of. Write down what he/she shares about your responses.

_____

_____

_____

_____

_____

_____

_____

_____

_____

_____

INTENTION

It is important to be intentional when you are creating the relationship you want. An intention is a commitment to carry out an action in the future. Being intentional about the relationship you are creating together can be a powerful tool in helping manifest outcomes in your relationship. If you do not set an intention, you are leaving your relationship up to chance and influence from outside friends, family, or circumstances. Long-lasting, healthy relationships do not work out *by chance.*

Your intentions do not have to be the same but should be ones that will help create a relationship that is healthy and fulfilling for both of you. My intention with my husband is "to have a harmonious relationship." Reminding myself of this helps me not argue with him. My husband's intention is "to provide for my wife and meet her needs." My husband does not like conflict, and I do not like financial stress. As we both stay committed to our individual intentions, we create a more stable marriage for each other.

Write down an intention that will help you create the relationship you desire.

_____

_____

_____

_____

_____

_____

_____

_____

_____

_____

_____

_____

_____

_____

_____

_____

_____

_____

Elisabeth Davies, M.C.

AFFIRMATION

In addition to being intentional about the relationship you are creating with your partner, repeating affirmations silently or out loud can help rewire what you think and believe about your relationship. An affirmation is a declaration that something is true. Changing negative thoughts and beliefs to positive ones will ultimately change the way you act and strengthen your ability to become your best self as a partner.

An affirmation I often repeat for my marriage is, "I am a loving wife." I have practiced stating this in my mind for many years. Over the past several years, my husband has said to me, "You are very loving." This validates for me that I have changed who I am as a wife. He never said this about me the first couple of years we were together!

Write an affirmation declaring who you are becoming as a partner in your relationship. Read it often and be intentional about becoming what you affirm.

_____

_____

_____

_____

_____

_____

_____

_____

_____

_____

_____

_____

_____

_____

_____

_____

_____

_____

Elisabeth Davies, M.C.

Chapter 2

See How You Score on the Couple's Relationship Quiz

Read this chapter together, then take the Couple's Relationship Quiz separately. Your scores will most likely be different. Share your completed quiz with each other to learn what your individual strengths are in your relationship.

Now that you have started discussing what a relationship means to you, you may notice that your partner has different ideas, experiences, and expectations than you do. I have noticed this to be true with most couples I have counseled. This has been my personal experience, too. My husband and I have parents who had very dissimilar marriages. You do not have to come from similar backgrounds to create a great relationship together, but it helps knowing your partner's background to understand their relationship values.

CLIENT STORY

Lana and George were clients who came to me with different backgrounds in relationship values. George watched his parents communicate through affection and Lana observed her parents communicate through talking. During their first counseling appointment, George complained about a lack of affection and intimacy from Lana, and Lana complained that George didn't talk things through.

"George gets frustrated with me when I want to talk about issues I am having with co-workers or sharing responsibility with our daughter. He thinks a hug is going to fix it, and it's not," Lana explained. Her irritation was evident.

I explained to George, "Oftentimes, women are more open to intimacy and affection if they feel emotionally connected to their partner, which can grow from listening to Lana when she is communicating so she feels heard and validated."

I explained to Lana that physical touch is often how men feel connected to their partner and physical closeness can increase as she practices initiating by holding hands, cuddling, hugging, and kissing George.

I gave them both separate homework to practice until their next appointment with me a week later. Every day, George was to ask Lana how her day went and listen, and Lana was to initiate touch every day with George. When George and Lana returned, they both reported progress with communication and physical closeness in their relationship.

Communication and affection are only two necessary foundations to building a strong relationship with each other. Taking the Couple's Relationship Quiz will help both of you identify the qualities that you bring to your relationship as well as the areas that need strengthening. It is not uncommon for your partner to see you differently than you see yourself in a relationship, so be open to feedback as you are both learning how to have a better relationship together.

COUPLE'S RELATIONSHIP QUIZ

Take this relationship quiz separately, then share your results with your partner so you can identify your relationship strengths and weaknesses. Mark the box that most applies.

RELATIONSHIP FOUNDATIONS	1 *Hardly Ever*	2 *Sometimes*	3 *Often*	4 *Always*
COMMITMENT — *I agree to stay in the relationship and work together to resolve all difficulties.*				
COMMUNICATION — *I clearly express my feelings, opinions, and needs. I allow my partner to do the same.*				
TRUST — *I demonstrate integrity by being honest, loyal, and faithful in my relationship.*				
RESPECT — *I value and honor my partner. I cooperate and show regard for his/her boundaries.*				
LOVE — *I consistently recognize the good in my partner and make choices that benefit his/her wellbeing.*				
AUTONOMY — *I am confident in who I am and can be myself in this relationship.*				
INTIMACY & AFFECTION — *I share myself physically and emotionally. I feel a deep connection to my partner.*				

Elisabeth Davies, M.C.

To calculate your score, add up the points associated with each answer's column, then look at the score ranges below to see how you did.

- Score 7 - 12: Poor relationship skills
- Score 13 - 18: Fair relationship skills
- Score 19 - 23: Good relationship skills
- Score 24 - 28: Great relationship skills

COUPLE'S JOURNAL

Answer these questions separately, then share your answers with each other.

1. What was your score on the Couple's Relationship Quiz? *(Example: poor relationship skills, fair relationship skills, good relationship skills)*

_____

_____

_____

_____

_____

_____

_____

_____

_____

2. What are your strengths? *(Example: Intimacy and Affection, Respect, Love)*

_____

_____

_____

_____

_____

_____

_____

_____

_____

3. What areas need improvement? *(Example: Trust, Commitment, Autonomy)*

_____

_____

_____

_____

_____

_____

_____

_____

_____

_____

4. What was your partner's feedback on your relationship quiz score? Did he/she agree or disagree with how you scored yourself?

_____

_____

_____

_____

_____

_____

_____

_____

_____

_____

_____

_____

COUPLE'S HOMEWORK

Pick one of the seven qualities where you gave yourself a score of 1 (hardly ever) or 2 (sometimes). Be intentional at getting better at this quality every day until you both notice improvement with it in your relationship.

Partner 1: One quality I will be working on is...

_____

_____

_____

_____

_____

_____

_____

_____

_____

_____

Partner Two: One quality I will be working on is...

_____

_____

_____

_____

_____

_____

_____

_____

_____

_____

_____

_____

_____

LOVE TIP

Commit to building a strong foundation of communication, trust, respect, and love with your partner so that your relationship remains strong through all of life's difficulties.

INTENTION

Our relationship grows in
communication, respect, trust, and love
as we commit to creating a closer relationship.

AFFIRMATION

I am a respectful communicator.
I am a trustworthy partner,
and I am affectionate with my partner.

TRUST COMMITMENT COMMUNICATION LOVE RESPECT INTIMACY & AFFECTION AUTONOMY

Elisabeth Davies, M.C.

Chapter 3

Foundations for Having a Healthy Relationship

Read this chapter together. Take time to discuss your thoughts, feelings, and opinions about your relationship.

Now that you have taken the Couple's Relationship Quiz and know the seven necessary components every relationship needs to thrive, let's discuss why this foundation is so important.

The foundation of a healthy relationship is like the foundation of a home. If your house is built on sand or dirt rather than on concrete or rock, what will happen to it over time, especially after storms or unpredictable weather? How long can it stand or be held together if it does not have a solid foundation?

The same is true for your relationship. If it is not built on a strong foundation of communication, love, commitment, trust, respect, autonomy, and intimacy, how long will it last or be held together when adversity, loss, or hardship strikes?

Just like solid cement or a rock foundation keeps a house in place, a strong foundation of communication, love, commitment, trust, respect, autonomy, and intimacy keeps a relationship securely held together. Once this foundation of your relationship is secure, your partnership can grow up into a healthy, long-lasting bond.

It is common to be strong in some of the seven core areas but not all. For example, if you are strong in love and commitment, but weak in trust, this will affect the respect you have for your partner and impact your intimacy and affection. One relationship foundation affects the other. The same is true of a cement foundation of a home. If there is a crack or two, with shifting, weather, and time, these can become bigger cracks, weakening the whole foundation.

CLIENT STORY

Patricia and Josh experienced this in their relationship. They came to me for marriage counseling because of Patricia's lack of trust. They had been married twenty-one years and had five children together, four still living at home.

They both said they were committed to keeping their marriage together and loved each other. Patricia said she did not trust Josh because she had caught him in several lies and fraudulent business practices. Patricia said when she had communicated these concerns to Josh, their communication worsened, and it caused more tension in their relationship.

Josh told me, "It's none of her business how I run my company! I pay the bills in the house. Why is it a big deal how I handle customers or where I travel for business?"

"See," Patricia said, looking at me. "This is the anger I get every time I ask why he lied to a customer on the phone or why he has to travel over the weekend for business. I don't think he is being faithful, either," she added.

"Oh my God! There you go again, accusing me of cheating." Josh angrily countered.

"Timeout," I called, holding my hands in the shape of a "T." I looked at Josh and asked, "How do you want Patricia to respond when she overhears a conversation with your client or when you travel for business on the weekend?"

"I want her to keep our marriage separate from my business," Josh answered.

"Is that possible?" I asked, looking at Patricia.

"Josh works out of the home sometimes when he is not traveling. It's hard to not overhear his conversations when I'm doing chores around the house during the day." Patricia said.

"Do you think you are honest in business and in your marriage?" I enquired, looking at Josh.

"I do what it takes to make it work." Josh said confidently.

"Does Patricia have any reason to not trust you?" I asked Josh.

"She doesn't believe me anyways, so why bother explaining things to her?" Josh asked.

"Will explaining things to Patricia help your marriage?" I challenged Josh. Josh looked at Patricia.

She responded, "You have a lot of explaining to do to get me to trust you again, Josh."

Josh let out a deep sigh.

"How about we start with just one incident that caused Patricia to doubt your word or behavior?" I suggested.

"Okay," said Patricia. "Where were you last Saturday? You said you would be home by three o'clock and you did not get home till six o'clock! Your phone went right to voicemail when I called at four o'clock and five o'clock.

When you got home, you said your phone had a dead battery and you were stuck in traffic. For three hours? Really? And you were on the phone when you came in the door, so how could your phone have a dead battery?"

"Oh my God!" Josh said heatedly. "Why do you have to know where I am all the time? I am a grown man! I do not need to be supervised or check in with you every hour about my whereabouts!"

Patricia looked at me and said, "See, this is what happens every time I question him. He blows up. I never get a straight answer. The more I ask, the angrier he becomes, until I drop it."

I looked at Josh. "Is that your tactic? You use anger to respond to Patricia's questions instead of answering her with the truth? The angrier you become, the more Patricia backs off, and you get to keep doing what you do without accountability to your marriage for your whereabouts."

Josh stared at me.

Patricia interrupted the silence. "That's exactly what happens." She started to cry.

"What do you think would happen if you told Patricia the truth when she asked you questions?" I asked, looking at Josh.

"It would probably cause worse problems," he slowly said. "She is so uptight about things."

I suggested separate homework for both of them.

"Patricia, can you make a commitment to just listen when you ask Josh about his whereabouts? Don't respond or engage in an argument until our next appointment."

"Yes," she said hesitantly.

"Josh, can you practice telling Patricia the truth if she asks you a question about your whereabouts until our next appointment?"

"I'll try," he faltered.

Eight days later, Josh and Patricia came back to counseling.

"How did your week go?" I asked.

Patricia started, "Well, Josh did good at telling me the truth. He was late coming home this week. I didn't call his phone either. When he got home, I asked him where he was. He said he stopped at a bar to watch football and have a few beers. I didn't say anything."

"Well, Josh, how do you think it went this week?" I asked.

"Better, I guess. I just think Patricia wants me home whenever I'm not working. I need time to myself and time to decompress with the guys after work."

I looked at Patricia. "Which do you prefer? A husband who comes home right after work, stressed because he hasn't had time to decompress? Or a husband who comes home later and doesn't take his anger and stress out on the family?"

"Why can't he decompress at home?" Patricia asked.

"Tell her, Josh," I encouraged.

"Oh my God!" Josh exclaimed, becoming agitated. "You're kidding me, right? We have four loud kids, a dog, and the music blaring in the background. It's a crazy house to come home to! Then you start in on me with your questions. I literally have to brace myself every time I walk in the front door!"

Patricia was quiet.

"How do you want your home to be when you come in after work?" I asked.

"Peaceful, for starters," Josh quickly responded.

"Is that realistic?" I asked both of them.

"I suppose we could ask the kids to be quiet the first half hour that Josh gets home," Patricia suggested.

I invited them to have a family meeting before their next appointment with me. "Have your children sit down with both of you and tell them how you want the noise level in the home to be when you come home from work. Ask for their cooperation in making it a home with more peace and less stress."

Two weeks later, they came back to counseling.

"How did the trust and communication go this week in your marriage?" I asked.

"Better," said Patricia. "During our family meeting, our sixteen-year-old told us that he blares his music to drown out our fighting. Our daughter said if Josh and I quit fighting the house would be more peaceful. It was hard for me to hear, but I knew the kids were right. It's difficult for me not to say anything to Josh when I think he is lying to me, but arguing isn't the solution, either. I want a healthy marriage and family."

Josh agreed. "Patricia and I both promised the kids we would not fight anymore while they were in the house because we all want to get along better. Our twelve-year-old said she would go on a bike ride with me when I was mad at her mom."

"That's wonderful," I remarked. "I love how your twelve-year-old gave you a great solution to managing your anger, Josh." I continued, "I'm proud of you, Patricia, for realizing that arguing is not the solution for healing trust.

If you think Josh is not being honest, I want you to say to him, 'It helps me build trust with you when you tell me the truth.'"

Over the next two months they were in counseling, Josh told Patricia the truth more and managed his anger through physical exercise. Patricia continued to focus on not judging Josh for how he ran his business. Her trust grew and she practiced not arguing with Josh, which added more harmony to their communication.

Communication, trust, and the other relationship foundations can be repaired and learned, regardless of the current state of your relationship. I explain how this can be done in the following chapters.

COUPLE'S JOURNAL

Answer these questions separately, then share them with your partner. Talk about the ways each of you are making your relationship foundation solid.

1. Which foundational quality are you strengthening each week in your relationship? *(Example: I am being more committed to my relationship. I am being more respectful when communicating with my partner. I am consistently more affectionate with my partner.)*

_____

_____

_____

_____

_____

_____

_____

_____

_____

_____

_____

_____

_____

2. How has working on foundational qualities enhanced your relationship? *(Example: My partner and I talk more. Our relationship has become closer. We fight less.)*

_____

_____

_____

_____

_____

_____

_____

_____

_____

_____

_____

_____

_____

_____

_____

_____

_____

_____

_____

_____

_____

_____

_____

_____

COUPLE'S HOMEWORK

Write down what you are doing this week to strengthen one of the seven foundations of your relationship. *(Example: If you are working on trust, you are practicing rigorous honesty that can be validated through facts and evidence.)*

Partner 1: This week, I am strengthening _____
in our relationship by...

_____
_____
_____
_____
_____
_____
_____
_____
_____
_____

Partner 2: This week, I am strengthening _____
in our relationship by...

_____
_____
_____
_____
_____
_____
_____
_____
_____
_____
_____

LOVE TIP

Practice becoming skilled in each of the relationship foundations so that you become an amazing partner in your relationship.

INTENTION

Together, we are building a solid foundation
of commitment, trust, respect,
communication, love, intimacy,
and autonomy in our relationship.

AFFIRMATION

I am committed to my partner,
I am trustworthy,
I am respectful,
I show love and affection to my partner.

Elisabeth Davies, M.C.

Elisabeth Davies, M.C.

Chapter 4

How Well Do You Communicate?

Read this chapter together. Take time to discuss your thoughts, feelings,
and opinions about communication with each other.

Let's start with communication, because without it, neither of you will be able to relate to your partner's needs or desires.

Healthy communication includes asking for what you need and desire from your partner, as well as sharing who you are and encouraging an open dialogue. Your mood and non-verbal cues are not enough to let your partner know what you need. Your partner cannot know your thoughts or feelings, or how to best get along with you if you do not verbally communicate this information.

When you do verbalize what is on your mind or heart, you deserve to be heard. How many times have you said, "I already told you that," or "We already discussed this. Please listen to me." Poor communication is one of the most complained-about problems that couples bring up in my counseling office. There are many reasons for this.

REASONS FOR POOR COMMUNICATION

- Your parents or role models were not healthy communicators.
- You are afraid of being vulnerable and sharing your true thoughts and feelings.
- You are afraid of being judged or not accepted for speaking your true thoughts and feelings.
- You do not feel comfortable talking about the specific topic being discussed.
- You do not trust the receiver with your information.
- You have communicated many times without effective results, so you stop trying.
- You lack confidence in accurately expressing what you are trying to say.
- You are a private person and prefer to keep your thoughts and feelings to yourself.

CLIENT STORY

Jim and Jane came to me for couple's counseling and shared that they needed help with their communication. They were not being heard or understood by each other. As I listened to them, Jim cut Jane off mid-sentence to say, "Jane is a nag and I tune her out because she says the same thing repeatedly."

Jane defensively replied, "I wouldn't have to repeat myself if you would just listen to me the first time!"

I called a timeout for a moment to ask, "How would your conversations go if you were both good communicators with each other?"

Jane was the first to respond: "Jim wouldn't tune me out and ignore me when I'm trying to talk to him."

Jim responded by shrugging and not saying anything.

"It is very helpful to imagine what healthy communication in your relationship *would* look like. This way it gives you a goal on what to work toward," I explained.

I invited Jane and Jim to both practice the Parroting Exercise to help them listen, stop interrupting, and communicate effectively. I have used this with many couples because it is so effective.

PARROTING EXERCISE

One partner starts by saying what they need, using only one or two sentences at a time. No interrupting allowed. When he/she is finished, the listening partner says, "What I hear you saying is..." and 'parrots,' or repeats back word for word what he/she heard. Once the communicating partner is satisfied with the listening partner repeating the words correctly, the listening partner gets a turn to communicate a sentence or two, so each partner has a chance to speak and be heard. You can continue this one person at a time for up to five minutes.

This is how it went when Jim and Jane practiced the parroting exercise in my counseling office:

Jim: *I need you not to repeat yourself over and over. I heard you the first time. Just because I don't say anything back doesn't mean I didn't hear you.*

Jane: *What I hear you saying is you need me to not repeat myself over and over. You heard me the first time even if you didn't say anything back to me.*

Jim: *Yes.*

Jane: *If I felt like you heard me Jim and were not ignoring me, I wouldn't repeat myself.*

Jim: *What I hear you saying is that if you felt like I heard you and was not ignoring you, you wouldn't repeat yourself.*

Jane: *Yes. Can I say one more thing?*

Jim: *Yes, you can say one more thing.*

Jane: *Could you please say, "I heard what you said," when I am speaking to you?*

Jim: *What I hear you saying is that you want me to say, "I heard what you said," when you are speaking to me.*

Jane: *Yes, that way I will know you heard me, and I won't feel ignored by you.*

Jim: *What I hear you saying is that if I say, "I heard what you said," you will know I heard you and you won't feel ignored by me.*

Jane: *Yes, thank you.*

Jim: *You're welcome.*

I asked Jim and Jane to practice the Parroting Exercise every day, picking one topic of communication to improve until their next appointment with me. They came back to my counseling office ten days later. Both reported they fought less, communicated more effectively, and Jane said she felt Jim was being a better listener.

If one of you struggles to verbally communicate and the lack of communication is causing distance in your relationship, let your partner know this. You might say, "It is important for me to have good communication with you. Is there a time you are available so we can build better communication between us?" Although it can be frustrating to be with someone who finds it challenging to communicate, it is important that you continue to make time to positively communicate together each day to ensure a solid foundation for a healthy relationship.

Communication is a must for closeness in your relationship, but how you do it is up to you. Some people prefer texting, emailing, letter-writing, calling, Facetiming, or talking in person. Decide what mode of communication works best for your relationship, as long as both of you are able to express your needs and desires and become better communicators with each other.

It is common for couples to have disagreements about certain topics, such as friends, finances, in-laws, parenting, religion, or politics. If you argue about the same topic over and over in your relationship, solution-oriented communication is needed. Remember to come up with solutions that are in your control. Trying to get your partner to change *is not* a solution that is in your control. Changing what you say or do or how you respond *is* a solution that is in your control. If you are angry, trying to control your partner, or manipulating to get your way, communication will not be received well because you are not considering what is best for the relationship. Try navigating sensitive or difficult subjects by using constructive words and being mindful of your tone.

Sometimes one partner is introverted and quiet while the other is talkative. Honor each other's personality and style of communicating. Be patient with yourself and your partner as you both become better communicators.

SKILLS THAT WILL ENHANCE YOUR COMMUNICATION

- *Be a good listener.* Do not interrupt or dismiss what your partner is saying. Listening encourages your partner to continue communicating with you. Remember, listening does not mean you agree with everything your partner is saying. By listening, you honor your partner's voice.
- *Be approachable and open to communicating.* Do not engage when you are angry, because you are likely to say harsh words that cause your partner to withdraw. If you are upset, take a break. Calm yourself down and then communicate. This gives you time to be clear on what you want to say, and you will be received better.
- *Give your partner your undivided attention when he/she is speaking to you.* Do not be on your phone, computer, or watching TV. This lets your partner know what he/she is saying is important to you.
- *Give your partner time to respond to what you are saying.* Do not monopolize the conversation. This allows for a dialogue and an exchange of thoughts between you.
- *Be polite and respectful when you are talking to your partner.* This demonstrates you value him/her as a person. He/she will be less likely to shut down when you are talking.
- *Stick to one topic at a time and organize your thoughts before you speak.* This will help you get your point across.
- *Pay attention to your partner's body language.* Be aware if your partner is becoming defensive or distressed. This allows you an opportunity to pause and give him/her time to process.
- *Choose constructive words that enhance or build your relationship.* Your words are powerful and sometimes unforgettable.

It is one thing to know what healthy communication looks like and another to exercise skills and *be* a healthy communicator.

Elisabeth Davies, M.C.

If you find yourself struggling with communication, try journaling. Write down what you want to say to organize your thoughts. Journaling also helps get emotions out onto paper so that when you have an important conversation, difficult feelings such as anger, frustration, hurt and disappointment will not impede the conversation.

You can also practice a conversation you would like to have in front of a mirror, before talking with your partner. This can help you decide what is important to say and keep the conversation on point.

Communicating well will reap many benefits in your relationship. Not only will it keep you both feeling close and connected, but it will also equip you to express new information that can empower more positive interactions. Healthy communication shapes how your partner sees you and leaves a lasting impression.

If one of you is unwilling to learn to be a better communicator, your relationship will suffer. Lack of healthy communication in a relationship leads to feeling disconnected, distant, and misunderstood by your partner and it discourages you from talking about what is important to you. If this is the case, you can get additional support with books, professional counseling, workshops, or webinars on communication.

COUPLE'S JOURNAL

Answer the following questions separately. Then, share your answers with each other. Each week, discuss the progress you are both making as communicators in your relationship.

1. What communication skills are you naturally good at? *(Example: listening, giving your partner your undivided attention, not interrupting)*

---

2. What communication skills would you like to improve? *(Example: paying attention to your partner's body language, speaking calmly, sticking to one topic at a time)*

_____

_____

_____

_____

_____

_____

_____

_____

_____

_____

_____

3. What does your partner do to enhance communication in the relationship? *(Example: He/She doesn't get angry when I share my opinions. He/She doesn't monopolize the conversation. He/She doesn't criticize my feelings.)*

_____

_____

_____

_____

_____

_____

_____

_____

_____

_____

_____

_____

4. What do you do to keep the lines of communication open in your relationship? *(Example: I'm approachable. I initiate conversations. I accept that my partner has opposite views.)*

_____

_____

_____

_____

_____

_____

_____

_____

_____

_____

_____

5. Some things I would like to do better are: *(Example: give my undivided attention when we are having a conversation. Ask questions in a non-accusing way. Not interrupt when my opinion is different.)*

_____

_____

_____

_____

_____

_____

_____

_____

_____

_____

_____

_____

_____

COUPLE'S HOMEWORK

Write down what you will do to build healthier communication with your partner. *(Example: I will practice listening more, I will not criticize his/her opinions, I will wait until I am calm before communicating)*

Partner 1

_____
_____
_____
_____
_____
_____
_____
_____
_____
_____
_____

Partner 2

_____
_____
_____
_____
_____
_____
_____
_____
_____
_____
_____
_____

Elisabeth Davies, M.C.

LOVE TIP

Take a temporary break or timeout if you are arguing with your partner to de-escalate tension. Come back when you have calmed yourself down.

Offer a solution to the argument. Ask your partner for his/her solution as well.

INTENTION

Our relationship grows
in respectful communication,
which allows us to share our needs and desires
with each other in healthy ways.

AFFIRMATION

I choose to communicate with
[partner's name]
in ways that enhance cooperation
in our relationship.

Elisabeth Davies, M.C.

Chapter 5

How Good Are You at Staying in Love?

*Read this chapter together. Take time to discuss your thoughts, feelings, and opinions
about love with each other.*

Have you ever been in a relationship where at the time you thought you were in love, but
once it ended you wondered, *Was that really love*? Your partner may have said, "I love you,"
but did you truly feel loved? Our words can lie, but our behavior always tells the truth
about who we are and how we feel about someone. It is what you *do* that proves you love
someone.

The evidence of real love enables you to persevere together during difficult times. It is
the ingredient that allows you to forgive and see the good in your partner. It is what bonds
you together long-term.

The qualities of real love are described below and are taken from the Bible in 1 Corinthians 13:4-7 (NIV):

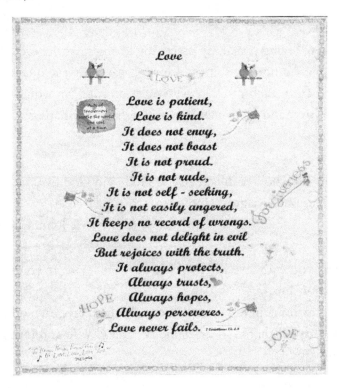

I keep these sixteen qualities of love where I can see them and read them often. They remind me to act in loving ways with my husband, myself, and those I love. If I say something rude, am being self-centered, or having trouble forgiving my husband, I can look at these qualities to prompt me to be intentional about practicing loving qualities.

CLIENT STORY

I went over these loving qualities with Bruce and Anna, who came to me for couple's counseling. They both said they loved each other. Anna struggled with trusting Bruce because she had been cheated on in two of her prior relationships. Bruce struggled with being patient with Anna because he was frustrated with her false accusations when she had no evidence that he would ever cheat on her. The lack of trust and patience in their relationship led to arguments. Both felt unloved.

I worked with Anna to stop falsely accusing Bruce without facts and evidence. I gave her exercises to help her forgive her past two suitors and heal her fear of infidelity. I helped Bruce be confident in his trustworthiness and not take Anna's words personally.

As Anna practiced trusting Bruce day by day and Bruce practiced being patient with Anna as she healed from being cheated on in her past, their love for each other was able to penetrate through former unhealed barriers. This resulted in a more loving relationship.

You can become a more loving person by practicing loving qualities each day. It is important to note that people are not the source of love; if we were, the qualities of love would instinctually flow out from each of us in every relationship. We would not hate anyone. God is the source of love, and God manifests through us, animating our hearts and ultimately our behavior.

> God is love, and all who live in love live in God, and God lives in them. And as we live in God, our love grows more perfect.
> — 1 John 4:16-17 (NLT)

Asking God to fill you with love will help you be more loving to yourself and to express this love in your relationship.

When I silently pray for couples, I ask God to help them love each other like God loves them. I also pray for myself that God helps me be a good wife and love my husband the way He loves my husband.

COUPLE'S JOURNAL

Answer the following questions separately. Then share them with your partner, to grow in love together as a couple.

1. What qualities of love do you exhibit regularly? *(Example: I am patient. I persevere through difficulties. I am honest.)*

_____

_____

_____

_____

_____

_____

_____

_____

_____

_____

2. What qualities of love do you desire more mastery in? *(Example: being less self-centered, not being rude, being less envious)*

_____

_____

_____

_____

_____

_____

_____

_____

_____

_____

_____

3. What qualities of love does your partner exhibit regularly? *(Example: He/She is forgiving, kind and protective.)*

_____

_____

_____

_____

_____

_____

_____

_____

_____

_____

_____

_____

4. Ask your partner what makes him/her feel loved in the relationship. Write down the response you received.

_____

_____

_____

_____

_____

_____

_____

_____

_____

_____

_____

Write down what you love about your partner and give this to him/her.

WHAT I LOVE ABOUT YOU

Date:

To: From:

I love that you...

_____

_____

_____

_____

_____

_____

_____

_____

_____

_____

_____

_____

_____

_____

_____

_____

_____

_____

_____

_____

_____

_____

_____

_____

Date:

To: From:

I love that you…

_____
_____
_____
_____
_____
_____
_____
_____
_____
_____
_____
_____
_____
_____
_____
_____
_____
_____
_____
_____
_____
_____
_____
_____
_____

COUPLE'S HOMEWORK

Read through the sixteen qualities of love together. Each of you pick one you need more mastery in. Practice that quality with your partner until you both notice it improving in your relationship.

Qualities of Love

1. Patient: *tolerant, uncomplaining*
2. Kind: *gracious, considerate, helpful*
3. Not jealous: *does not envy others or what they have*
4. Not boastful: *does not brag and is not arrogant*
5. Not proud: *humble, modest about personal achievements*
6. Not rude: *polite and respectful to others*
7. Does not demand their own way: *benevolent, accommodating, compromising*
8. Not irritable: *good humored, easy-going*
9. Keeps no record of being wronged: *forgiving, merciful to others*
10. Does not delight in evil: *practices what is right and good*
11. Rejoices with the truth: *consistently honest, shows integrity*
12. Always protects: *guards and defends others from harm*
13. Always trusts: *assured, certain about truth*
14. Always hopes: *anticipates positive outcomes*
15. Always perseveres: *endures through every circumstance, never quits*
16. Never fails: *constant and forever*

LOVE TIP

Write down what you love about your partner and give this to him/her.

INTENTION

I open my heart to receive
all the love that is available for me.

AFFIRMATION

As I am filled with love, I allow this love to flow to
[partner's name],
for I know love is endless in its capacity to be expressed.

Elisabeth Davies, M.C.

Chapter 6

Committing for Longevity

Read this chapter together. Take time to discuss your thoughts, feelings, and opinions about commitment.

Commitment is a necessary foundation to building a lasting relationship because it is the superglue that holds a relationship together. It only takes one person to give up on the relationship — emotionally or physically — for it to deteriorate.

Commitment means two people agree to stay in the relationship and work together to resolve all difficulties throughout their lifetime. This can be a scary thought for any number of reasons. Perhaps you are afraid of being held accountable in your relationship. Maybe it's scary to commit to one partner if you have expectations he/she doesn't meet, or you could want a way out if things do not go as you planed.

Divorce is at an all-time high in the United States, and many couples are choosing to live together rather than marry. There is less commitment and risk this way.

I like to use the parenting relationship as an example of what it looks like to stay committed during difficult times. A dedicated parent stays in their child's life and raises their child even when that child makes it difficult. Children may not follow rules. They may be disrespectful or make choices that infuriate us. We don't say, "That's it! I won't be your parent anymore!"

As a counselor, I have encountered many clients who have left and not maintained relationships with their children or their partner. Relationships are work. Leaving a child or a committed relationship does not prepare you to be more committed in the next relationship. Being a healthy partner or parent takes skill, effort, and perseverance, all of which can be practiced and implemented so that your relationship can proceed.

We all can be difficult at times, making it hard on others to be in a relationship with us. This is a good time to take mini breaks or timeouts to destress and recalibrate our perspective. Go for a walk or take a drive. Pray that God helps you to be a good partner. Talk to a trusted friend who will strengthen you so you can reset your thoughts and feelings. Then, come back into the relationship with the intention that whatever was challenging you will be resolved together so that the relationship remains intact.

If you are in a relationship with a partner who lacks concern for your wellbeing because they are physically abusive, verbally abusive, unfaithful, or have addictive behavior that makes it impossible to thrive, this is not healthy. It is your responsibility to stand up for yourself, set healthy boundaries, and remove yourself from people who display destructive behavior toward you. If your partner is not willing to take action that causes positive, permanent change, I recommend you seek psychological and spiritual advice from qualified experts to determine if it is in the best interest of both of you to stay in the relationship.

If your partner does care about your wellbeing, threatening to leave makes it almost impossible for him/her to get close to you because it is not safe to give your heart to someone who threatens to leave you. Threatening to leave your partner weakens the foundation of commitment because the fear of being abandoned will grow and he/she will have to protect himself/herself from being deserted.

Other behaviors that fracture or weaken commitment in a relationship include filing for divorce, abandoning, or cutting off communication. These scenarios send a strong message to your partner: "I do not value you enough to stay and work through difficulties with you."

CLIENT STORY

Roberta and James struggled with commitment for years in their marriage. Roberta moved out on James after they had been married twelve years. She moved back in with him six months later when they started seeing me for counseling.

Roberta shared with me, "I found out James cheated on me, so I left, and I had an affair."

"Are you still legally married?" I asked, looking at both of them.

"Yes," James said.

"Do you forgive each other for the affairs?" I inquired.

"I forgive Roberta," James responded. "But she brings up my affair almost every argument we get in, no matter how many times I have apologized for it and have stayed faithful ever since."

"I would have never cheated on you if you didn't cheat on me first!" Roberta justified.

"Do two wrongs make it right?" I asked Roberta.

"No, I guess not," she answered.

"Are you willing to forgive James?" I asked her.

"Yes, but I'm not having sex with him again," Roberta said defiantly.

"Well, how is your marriage going to work?" I asked her. "Sex is important because it is needed for closeness, connection, and intimacy. Who is going to meet James's needs if you refuse?"

"He can take care of himself!" Roberta flippantly replied.

"If you really forgave James for the affair, then you wouldn't continue to bring it up in arguments or refuse to be intimate with him. I think you are still hurt, Roberta." I countered.

"The past is the past…" Roberta trailed off.

"James, I want you to ask Roberta if there is anything you can say or do to help her heal from your affair," I suggested.

James asked Roberta and she replied, "I don't know."

James looked at Roberta. "You can't keep moving in and moving out," he told her. "One day you pretend like everything is fine, then a week later you threaten to move out again. One night you spend the night on the couch and another night you ask me to sleep on the couch so you can sleep in our bed. I cannot keep being jerked around. You need to make up your mind. Either you are committed to working on our marriage or you're not."

"Don't give me ultimatums, James!" Roberta said, raising her voice.

I asked both of them if they would be willing to be committed to their marriage during the time they were in counseling with me.

They both agreed.

I reiterated, "This means no threatening to leave or break up or divorce while you are continuing counseling."

For homework, I asked Roberta to practice the forgiveness exercise. Each time she thought about James's affair, I told her to counter those thoughts by saying, "I unconditionally forgive James for having an affair."

I explained to Roberta, "Forgiving James doesn't take away the fact that James's affair was wrong. Forgiveness releases your hurt, bitterness, anger, and negative emotions that grow as you harbor the affair."

I gave James homework to write down what he thinks makes a good husband and to focus on what is in his control. I explained, "What Roberta says and does is not in your control."

Twelve days later, they came back to counseling.

"How is the commitment going in the marriage this week?" I asked as our counseling session began.

"Great," started James. "I have always been committed to staying married to Roberta."

"James has been a lot nicer to me," Roberta commented. "It was easier to forgive him this past week."

James shared what he thought makes a good husband: "Be supportive.

Provide for my wife and our three children. Be a good friend to Roberta. Work as a team, together. Love her."

I asked Roberta what she thought makes a good wife. "Be supportive. Be a team player; make decisions together. Be respectful," she replied.

I encouraged them to practice being the best husband and wife to each other every day as they continued to work on healing through their affairs and repairing fractured commitment in their marriage.

SKILLS TO REPAIR COMMITMENT

1. Sincerely apologize to your partner for breaking commitment by threatening to leave or divorce. Let him/her know how you are going to strengthen the commitment you have in your relationship.
2. When you feel like leaving because the relationship has become intolerable to you, take a break. Go for a drive, a walk, or do something that calms and de-escalates you. Let your partner know you will be back when you are calm.
3. Seek guidance from those who support your relationship being healthy, like a pastor, counselor, friend, or family member.
4. Continue to practice and learn ways on how to stay committed so you become skilled in this area.
5. Bring effective solutions to the relationship when disagreements or conflicts arise. List ways you can make the relationship more bonded. Share these ideas with your partner and ask what his/her solutions are to strengthen commitment. One solution may be to practice not taking your partner's words or behaviors personally or to practice more patience and kindness in your interactions.
6. Talk to other couples who have long-term relationships. Ask them what their secret is to staying committed in their relationship.

My ability to stay with my husband — through hardships, emotional hurt, and weariness — comes from the relationship I have with God, who stays with me even though I have made so many mistakes and poor choices over the years. This Bible verse encourages me:

So be strong and courageous! Do not be afraid and do not panic before them. For the Lord your God will personally go ahead of you. He will neither fail you nor abandon you.

— Deuteronomy 31:6 (NLT)

Knowing that God will never abandon me encourages me to stay in relationship with the people He loves and who I love.

COUPLE'S JOURNAL

Answer the following questions separately. Then, share your answers with your partner. Check in with each other every week to share the progress you are both making to strengthen commitment in your relationship.

1. How do you let your partner know you are committed to the relationship? *(Example: working through arguments, forgiving him/her, staying in the relationship)*

_____

_____

_____

_____

_____

_____

_____

2. Have you said or done things in the past that made you or your partner doubt your commitment to the relationship? *(Example: threatening to leave, being in another intimate relationship while you are in a relationship with your partner, cutting off communication)*

_____

_____

_____

_____

_____

_____

_____

_____

3. How does your partner let you know he/she is committed to staying in a relationship with you? *(Example: He/She is loyal. He/She does not threaten to leave. He/She talks about future plans for us.)*

_____

_____

_____

_____

_____

_____

_____

_____

_____

_____

4. Has your partner said or done things in the past that weakened the commitment to your relationship? *(Example: He/She said they would leave when the kids were grown. He/She spends quality time with others but does not spend time with me. He/She makes little effort to get close and deeply connect with me.)*

_____

_____

_____

_____

_____

_____

_____

_____

_____

_____

Elisabeth Davies, M.C.

COUPLE HOMEWORK

Write a thank you letter to your partner for staying with you and supporting the relationship during times of difficulty (grief and loss, financial hardship, raising kids, in-law problems, career change, illness, arguments). Give this letter to him/her.

Date:

To: From:

Thank you for staying with me and persevering through our relationship when…

_____

_____

_____

_____

_____

_____

_____

_____

_____

_____

_____

_____

_____

_____

_____

_____

_____

_____

_____

_____

_____

_____

Date:

To: From:

Thank you for staying with me and persevering through our relationship when…

_____

_____

_____

_____

_____

_____

_____

_____

Elisabeth Davies, M.C.

LOVE TIP

Tell your partner that having a relationship with him/her is important to you. Let him/her know you are committed to working through difficulties together. Share what actions you are taking to deepen the commitment you have for him/her.

INTENTION

Our relationship perseveres
through all of life's trials.

AFFIRMATION

My love for
[partner's name]
grows as I commit to staying
on this journey together.

Chapter 7

Building Trust with Your Partner

Read this chapter together. Take time to discuss your thoughts, feelings, and opinions about trust.

Trust allows your partner to have confidence in what you say and do and to know that you are loyal to the relationship. Trust means demonstrating integrity by being honest and faithful in your relationship and being transparent with daily decisions.

If you do not trust, it means you do not believe your partner (or someone else) has your highest good in mind. Trust issues develop when you are lied to, cheated on, betrayed, or grow up with parents or caretakers who do not follow through with what they say. Because this happens to many people, trust issues are prevalent in relationships.

Unhealed trust issues will impede your ability to be vulnerable, which is essential for deep connection. It also impairs your ability to commit in a relationship out of fear of betrayal (less risk of you being hurt). A relationship without trust is never rewarding or fulfilling and is destined to remain shallow.

Fortunately, trust issues can be healed. You will learn ten strategies to heal trust later in this chapter. If you have trust issues, it is important to heal them because trust determines how you respond to each other. If you assume, accuse, or question your partner's character without having factual, supportive evidence, you likely wrestle with trust issues.

Trust goes both ways in a relationship. You and your partner should feel comfortable being vulnerable because this is the pathway to connection, honesty, and intimacy. Both of you are responsible for making it safe for truth to be shared without judgment, ridicule, or negative consequence. Nobody wants to be judged for sharing how they feel or who they are.

CLIENT STORY

Felicia had prior trust issues when she and Leroy began couple's counseling. They had been married one year. Felicia had been married twice before and those unions ended due to domestic violence. She had been single six years before marrying Leroy. He had never been married before but was living with the mother of his nine-year-old daughter when they met.

Their counseling sessions were initiated because Leroy had difficulty with time management. He told Felicia he was going to be home from work at 4 p.m. and repeatedly arrived twenty to thirty minutes late. Because her trust issues were unhealed, she would assume Leroy was cheating on her or somewhere he was not supposed to be. Leroy swore he never cheated on Felicia and gave her full access to his emails and text messages to prove he was trustworthy. Felicia remained suspicious until she addressed the hurt from her past that was obscuring how she was responding in her current relationship. Although it was not in Leroy's control to heal Felicia's trust issues, her false accusations and questioning of his character caused him to become angry, resentful, and distant in their marriage.

I invited Felicia to ask herself, "Where is the evidence for non-trusting thoughts, beliefs, or accusations?" This helped her discern whether her feelings and fears were truly a violation of trust incurred by Leroy, or an unhealed trust issue rooted in her past. I also suggested she practice daily forgiveness exercises, by saying in her mind, "I unconditionally forgive my ex-husbands for betraying my trust." Over time, this helped heal the betrayals from her prior marriages. Until Felicia's trust issues from the past were healed, they would spill over into her relationship with Leroy and sabotage her from having a successful marriage.

I gave Leroy homework too. He was to stop taking Felicia's trust issue's personally and stop trying to prove his trustworthiness, instead telling her, "It hurts me that you are unwilling to acknowledge I am trustworthy. I would like an apology for your false accusations." I also suggested he text his wife if he was going to be late. This would show consideration for his relationship.

After about six intense counseling sessions, Felicia had become significantly more forgiving, Leroy was remarkably less angry and better at time management, and they both talked to each other more lovingly.

If you lie, cheat, steal, or are disloyal in your relationship, it is impossible for your partner to depend on you as a trustworthy person, because each time you get caught in untrustworthy behavior, you erode the foundation of your relationship, leaving your partner to wonder, *What else will you hide or lie about?* and trust begins to deteriorate.

Besides lying and other untrustworthy behavior, having an unhealthy dependency or addiction also creates trust issues in a relationship. Millions of Americans have an unhealthy dependency that impairs their ability to be fully present to create a healthy relationship.[iii] Overconsumption of alcohol, drugs, gambling, pornography, shopping, food, internet gaming, and working are just a few examples of common addictions.

Addiction steals our time and focus and must be worked on before trust is possible because symptoms of addiction include hiding, sneaking, lying about the use, or participation in the unhealthy dependency.

All human beings have been dishonest about something at least once in their life. In fact, I have never heard anyone say, "Trust human beings; you will never be let down or betrayed!"

Just as we are not the source of love, we are not the source of trust; otherwise, all people would be inherently trustworthy.

> This is what the Lord says: Cursed are those who put their trust in mere humans, who rely on human strength and turn their hearts away from the Lord.
> — Jeremiah 17:5 (NLT)

> But blessed are those who trust in the Lord and have made the Lord their hope and confidence.
> — Jeremiah 17:7 (NLT)

I have seen many relationships dissolve because trust continued to be broken through ongoing lying, infidelity, overspending, or continued addiction. I have also counseled hundreds of couples with fractured trust in their relationship who have used the strategies below to successfully repair their partnerships.

EFFECTIVE WAYS TO HEAL TRUST ISSUES

- See your trust issue as self-sabotaging rather than self-protective. Unhealed trust issues will not block future hurt; instead, they will sabotage every relationship you have. All people are imperfect. You will most likely be hurt and you will accidentally hurt others.
- There is no hurt you cannot heal from if you practice forgiving everyone who has wronged you. Allow for mistakes and more opportunities for people to be honest. Do not bring up what your partner has already apologized for. God extends forgiveness to us each time we make mistakes. Ask Him to help you do the same.
- Trust is *earned*. Start off with an open mind and extend trust to new people as they build a track record with you.

- Practice rigorous honesty so that you become more trustworthy. Apologize when you are dishonest and let your partner know how you are going to correct your behavior.
- Make it safe for your partner to be honest with you by not judging, criticizing, or yelling at him/her for their choices. This will help him/her to be more open with you.
- Do not take it personally when your partner lies to you. Their dishonesty is their own shortcoming to work on. It is not about you.
- Be mindful of how your words and behaviors affect your partner so you do not further damage your trust. Know the undeniable facts and evidence before making accusations.
- Make choices that are for the highest good of the relationship rather than choices that only benefit you. This is key in repairing trust.
- Ask God to heal your trust issue and help you become a trustworthy person.

In order to be a trustworthy partner, you must speak truth without fear of how it will be received. You must be bold in integrity, even if it is not popular. Deciding to be a trustworthy partner demonstrates character and requires intentional accountability for your words and behaviors.

The rewards for being trustworthy are high esteem, respect, and confidence that you feel about yourself and that your partner can see in you, resulting in building a strong foundation for your relationship to flourish.

> Who can find a virtuous and capable wife? She is more precious than rubies. Her husband can trust her, and she will greatly enrich his life. She brings him good, not harm, all the days of her life.
>
> — Proverbs 31:10-12 (NLT)

> Better is a poor man who walks in his integrity than a rich man who is dishonest in his ways.
>
> — Proverbs 28:6 (NLT)

COUPLE'S JOURNAL

Answer the following questions separately. Then, share your answers with your partner to be more vulnerable and allow for deeper connection in your relationship.

1. Do you have any unhealed trust issues that spill over into your current relationship? *(Example: I falsely accuse my partner without evidence. I have difficulty being vulnerable with my partner. I am suspicious of my partner's behavior.)*

_____

_____

_____

_____

_____

_____

_____

_____

_____

_____

2. How have you demonstrated you are a trustworthy partner? *(Example: I am transparent about my unhealthy dependencies. I follow through with what I say. I am honest when I share my feelings and opinions.)*

_____

_____

_____

_____

_____

_____

_____

_____

_____

_____

3. Have you said or done anything that affects your partner's ability to trust you? *(Example: I lied to my partner. I cheated and hid emails or texts with inappropriate content. I was dishonest about my feelings.)*

_____

_____

_____

_____

_____

_____

_____

_____

_____

_____

_____

_____

4. Has your partner said or done anything that has betrayed your trust? *(Example: My partner was verbally or physically abusive to me. I found out information that my partner was hiding from me. My partner did not follow through with a promise he/she made.)*

_____

_____

_____

_____

_____

_____

_____

_____

_____

_____

_____

_____

5. What have you done to strengthen the trust in your relationship? *(Example: I have been honest about difficult topics. I have been loyal. I have not doubted my partner's intentions.)*

_____

_____

_____

_____

_____

_____

_____

_____

_____

_____

_____

_____

_____

_____

_____

_____

_____

_____

_____

_____

_____

_____

_____

_____

_____

_____

_____

_____

_____

COUPLE HOMEWORK

Write down things that have helped you build trust with your partner and share it with him/her.

Date:

To: From:

Some things you did that helped me trust you more…

_____

_____

_____

_____

_____

_____

_____

_____

_____

_____

_____

_____

_____

_____

_____

_____

_____

_____

_____

_____

_____

_____

_____

Elisabeth Davies, M.C.

Date:

To: From:

Some things you did that helped me trust you more…

_____

_____

_____

_____

_____

_____

_____

_____

_____

_____

_____

_____

_____

_____

_____

_____

_____

_____

_____

_____

_____

_____

_____

LOVE TIP

Let your partner know that building a foundation of trust in your relationship is important to you. Share that you are willing to practice more grace and forgiveness for past mistakes (yours and his/hers) so you can experience a safe relationship where both of you are vulnerable with each other for deeper connection and intimacy.

INTENTION

I am building a trustworthy relationship
as I operate from honesty and integrity.

AFFIRMATION

I choose to trust
[partner's name]
knowing that my relationship
should be given new chances
to build a foundation
practiced in honesty, loyalty, and faithfulness.

Elisabeth Davies, M.C.

Elisabeth Davies, M.C.

Chapter 8

Are You Respectful in Your Relationship?

Read this chapter together. Take time to discuss your thoughts, feelings, and opinions about respect.

Your partner will not feel cherished if your communication and behavior is not respectful. Respect is essential to building a healthy relationship, which means having regard for who your partner is and esteeming them in your interactions. It includes treating your partner with honor, acknowledging his/her value and showing cooperation, accepting the boundaries that he/she sets with you, caring about what is important to him/her, and recognizing that he/she is a valuable person, not just a means to get something you want.

Disrespecting your partner will put barriers in your relationship and cause hurt, resentment, and a lack of closeness. For example, if your partner flirts with your best friend in front of you or makes a joke at your expense, you may feel he/she is not on your team and withdraw.

You will lose respect for your partner each time he/she uses words that devalue you or behaves in a way that shows a lack of regard for you. These behaviors include broken promises, yelling or screaming, failing to follow through with responsibilities, self-centered choices, lack of self-control, lack of character or integrity, and shunning accountability by blaming someone else for your words or behavior.

If you are in a relationship with a partner who is disrespectful, it is important to share when you feel disrespected so that he/she knows and has an opportunity to behave differently. It is also important to teach your partner how you want him/her to talk to you and behave so he/she can learn to practice treating you in ways that make you feel respected. You may say something along the lines of, "It is disrespectful to yell at me and degrade me. I need you to talk to me calmly and talk to me like I am valuable and loved by you. If you continue this behavior, I am not going to be around you until you can be respectful."

It is your responsibility to teach others how to treat you, even though it may seem uncomfortable teaching another adult how to interact with you in a respectful way. A partner who is disrespectful most likely was raised in a household where he/she was disrespected. He/she may have been yelled at or mistreated by parents or family members. He/she may have witnessed parents or caretakers getting away with being disrespectful to each other as well.

If you let others devalue you, you do not respect yourself. People will continue to disrespect you if you allow it, and you will continue to experience contemptuous relationships. Respect is learned and can be cultivated at any time, but first you must respect yourself.

WAYS TO GAIN SELF-RESPECT

- Practice good self-care. Eat healthy, exercise at least thirty minutes each day, drink a lot of water, and be kind to yourself with your thoughts.
- Make daily choices that help you reach your full potential. Share your gifts and talents with others.
- Express spiritual qualities with others daily: love, peace, joy, kindness, patience, generosity, faithfulness, goodness, and self-control.
- Stand up for what you believe is right and good.
- Speak to others how you want to be spoken to. Do not use profanity, derogative statements, or bad-mouth others.
- Follow through with what you agree to do.
- Do your best at everything you do.
- Manage your emotions by choosing thoughts that enhance your mood.

Finally, brothers and sisters, whatever is true, whatever is noble, whatever is right, whatever is pure, whatever is lovely, whatever is admirable-if anything is excellent or praiseworthy-think about such things.

— Philippians 4:8 (NLT)

In other words, think about what is good and right. Let those thoughts dominate the lens through which you see the world.

Once you have self-respect, you will be able to treat your partner and others respectfully.

CLIENT STORY

Larry and Amanda were an older couple who were Catholic and belonged to a generation that believed divorce is not an option, even though their daughter, Emily, had suggested it to them on several occasions. Emily drove them to my counseling office because she was tired of getting regular phone calls from her parents to break up their fights.

Larry was a retired army veteran and Amanda was a retired bar and restaurant owner. Larry called Amanda an "idiot" during our first session and she reacted by calling him a "bastard." I told them, "I do not allow name calling during counseling sessions. If you do it, I will call a timeout. If you continue, I will end the session." They tried to have respectful communication with one another in front of me, but the years of ongoing verbal abuse, threatening to harm each other, and even hate were evident.

Over several sessions, I gave Larry and Amanda homework exercises to practice new skills with each other outside of the counseling office. I asked them to write down what they needed from their spouse as well as what kind of a spouse they wanted to be. Amanda's request was simple. She wanted Larry to be kind, provide for her financially, and get her to her doctors' appointments. Larry wanted Amanda to cook for him every day, do his laundry, have sex with him, not argue with him and find her own ride to her doctors' appointments. Neither of them identified what kind of a spouse they wanted to be. They were focused on their own needs, not giving to one another or their marriage.

When Larry and Amanda started complaining about the other, I asked, "What kind of a person do *you* want to be? You cannot change your spouse, but you can respond to your spouse in a way that you believe is your best self, and this will change your relationship."

I told them both to take a break from each other if a fight was eminent. Instead of calling their daughter, I suggested they take a time out from each other and go for a walk around the retirement home alone or sit outside. During this time, they were to silently say in their mind, "I forgive my spouse for saying or doing [behavior]," until they noticed their anger dissipate. Once calmer, they were to ask themselves, "How can I respond to this situation in a way that would make me proud of myself?"

If you find yourself arguing or disrespecting your partner, try answering these questions: How would you respond to this situation if you were a loving person? How would you respond to this situation if you desired peace in your relationship? How would you respond to this situation if you were a kind person? How would you respond to this situation if you were a gentle person?"

Amanda was better at practicing the counseling homework than Larry, and the relationship did get better. There was less fighting when Amanda took more walks and didn't yell back when Larry was belittling her. She started spending more time with family and friends. Before the ninth session, Emily called to thank me because her parents had stopped calling her to break up their fights.

EFFECTIVE SKILLS TO BUILD RESPECT BACK INTO YOUR RELATIONSHIP

- Tell your partner each time you feel disrespected, so he/she is aware of what words and behaviors are disrespectful to you, specifically.
- If your partner continues to be disrespectful, let him/her know you will not be in their presence until they choose to be respectful. This will protect you from being disrespected and allow for a healthier relationship.
- Apologize each time you have been disrespectful to your partner and tell him/her your plan on how you will be more respectful in the future.
- Say in your mind, "I forgive [partner's name]," when you remember what your partner said or did that felt disrespectful to you. This helps release old hurts and resentments from the past.
- Intentionally look for the positive qualities in your partner and verbalize these qualities to him/her daily. This will help change your perception of him/her and allow for more positive interaction.
- Demonstrate integrity daily by being honest, faithful, and considerate of the impact your words and behaviors have on your relationship.
- If you catch yourself wanting to say something mean or disrespectful, practice saying nothing until you can say something that enhances your relationship.
- Record your emotions in a journal. Exercise, or talk to a supportive person instead so you can be more in-control of your words.
- Take timeouts if you are angry or frustrated. Deescalate yourself. Do what calms you and puts you in a better mood.
- Remember that each word and behavior from your partner is evidence of who he/she is in that moment. His/her words and behavior are not a statement about you. Practice not taking your partners words and behaviors personally. He/she is accountable.
- Be intentional about what kind of a partner you want to be. Focus on yourself and responding in ways that make you proud of yourself.

Not only does your relationship get healthier when you are a respectful partner, but your friendship and connection also deepen. Being a respectful partner demonstrates that you value yourself and others. It also proves you have self-control and can manage your words and your emotions. It shows you have character and that you do not take other people's words and behavior personally.

COUPLE'S JOURNAL

Ask your partner the following questions and record your partner's responses. Share ways your partner can be more respectful, and your relationship can grow in respectful interactions.

1. Have I said or done things that made you feel disrespected by me? *(Example: lied, yelled, wrongfully accused you)*

_____

_____

_____

_____

_____

_____

_____

_____

_____

_____

2. How can I be more respectful to you in our relationship? *(Example: Use kind words. Be considerate of your likes and dislikes. Refrain from saying negative comments about your family or friends.)*

_____

_____

_____

_____

_____

_____

_____

_____

_____

3. Is there anything disrespectful I have done in the past that you have not forgiven me for? *(Example: degrading words, infidelity, poor follow-through on promises)*

_____

_____

_____

_____

_____

_____

_____

4. What can we both do to heal the lack of respect in our relationship? *(Example: Forgive the past. Have compassion with each other. Be loyal to each other.)*

_____

_____

_____

_____

_____

_____

_____

5. Do you consider yourself to be respectful as a partner? What is your evidence? *(Example: I keep my promises. I am not critical. I do not say or do things that are damaging to our relationship.)*

_____

_____

_____

_____

_____

_____

6. What are the ways you show respect for each other? *(Example: We use kind words and are not demanding when we need each other's help. We are considerate of each other. We appreciate our differences and do not try to control each other.)*

_____

_____

_____

_____

_____

_____

_____

_____

_____

_____

_____

_____

7. What do you respect most about yourself as a partner? *(Example: I follow through on my commitments. I always do my best. I overcome challenges and difficulties.)*

_____

_____

_____

_____

_____

_____

_____

_____

_____

_____

_____

_____

COUPLE HOMEWORK

Write down what you respect about each other and share it with your partner.

Date:

To: From:

Some things I respect about you are...

_____

_____

_____

_____

_____

_____

_____

_____

_____

_____

_____

_____

_____

_____

_____

_____

_____

_____

_____

_____

_____

_____

_____

Elisabeth Davies, M.C.

Date:

To: From:

Some things I respect about you are…

_____

_____

_____

_____

_____

_____

_____

_____

_____

_____

_____

_____

_____

_____

_____

_____

_____

_____

_____

_____

_____

_____

_____

_____

_____

How did it feel to hear what your partner respects about you?

_____

_____

_____

_____

_____

_____

_____

_____

_____

_____

_____

_____

How did your partner respond when you shared what you respect about him/her?

_____

_____

_____

_____

_____

_____

_____

_____

_____

_____

_____

_____

_____

Elisabeth Davies, M.C.

LOVE TIP

Let your partner know how important it is for you to feel respected by him/her.

Share what is acceptable and what is not acceptable treatment so that you both can build a relationship together that honors each other.

INTENTION

Our relationship continually grows in respect.

AFFIRMATION

I respectfully acknowledge
[partner's name]'s
life and love as a blessing to me.

Chapter 9

Autonomy in Your Relationship

Read this chapter together as a couple. Take time to discuss your individual personality traits, dreams, values, and goals that make you who you are. Share with your partner how his/her unique qualities attracted you to him/her.

Now that you have read and are practicing five of the components of a strong foundation for your relationship, let's move on to other ingredients that are necessary for a fulfilling and enjoyable relationship with your partner: autonomy, intimacy and affection, passion and romance, deep friendship, and adventure together.

Each of us are born with unique personalities, appearances, and qualities that make us who we are. Autonomy is the freedom to be your unique self and express who you are as a whole, distinct person. An autonomous person acts on his/her own values and morals and is not controlled or coerced to behave or think differently than who he/she is intrinsically.

You must have a sense of self-worth and self-respect to be autonomous. These are developed in childhood. If you were born into a family that did not love and accept you for who you are or did not make you feel you belonged in your family, you may have lost your sense of autonomy, suppressing your true self, to get your basic emotional needs of love, acceptance, and belonging met. If you were not encouraged to be your true self, you are likely to have experienced fear, self-doubt, insecurity, lack of self-esteem, or neediness in your relationships growing up.

If left unhealed, these deficiencies about your value can transfer over into your adult relationships and create a dynamic where you continuously look to your partner to reassure you and validate your worth. If you are relying on your partner for confidence to feel "good enough" or "complete" as a valuable human being, you are likely codependent. This means you lack the internal ability to create self-confidence, and instead rely on a relationship to validate your worth and to function at your full potential.

The purpose of a relationship is not to have a partner who completes you, but to share your completeness; to enhance each other. Therefore, it is paramount to love and accept yourself and be autonomous.

Below is an Autonomy Inventory you can both take to find out how you score when it comes to autonomy in your relationship.

AUTONOMY INVENTORY

Directions: Mark the box that most applies to you. Share your score with your partner to encourage autonomy in your relationship.

AUTONOMY QUALITIES	1 *Always*	2 *Sometimes*	3 *Rarely*
ACT ON MY OWN VALUES — *I make decisions based on my own morals and values. I am free of external control or manipulation of others.*			
INDEPENDENT — *I am not influenced by what other people think or say about me. I know my value comes from my inherent abilities.*			
SELF-RESPECT — *I act in ways that are aligned with integrity and goodness. I encourage myself to do what is right.*			
EMPOWERED — *I am intelligent and confident that I can learn new things and create a meaningful life through my own choices.*			
INDIVIDUAL — *I know myself and honor what I need. I engage in practices that enhance my development as a human being.*			
ASSERTIVE — *I ask for what I need. I let others know how to treat me. I stand up for myself if someone is devaluing me.*			
SELF-GOVERNING — *I take responsibility for my own thoughts, feelings, and beliefs. I am self-determined and accountable for my behavior.*			
SELF-ACCEPTING — *I forgive myself easily when I make mistakes. I accept that I am imperfect and lovable.*			
HEALTHY RELATIONSHIPS — *I am comfortable with myself when meeting new people or in new situations. I set healthy boundaries in my relationships.*			
SELF-CARE — *I make choices that are beneficial to my well-being: mind, body, and spirit. I take time each day to soothe and regulate my emotions and behaviors.*			

Add up your points on the Autonomy Inventory.

If you scored a 10, you have *good autonomy* in your relationship. Keep loving and believing in yourself!

If you scored 11 - 20, you have *fair autonomy* in your relationship and need to incorporate more autonomy builders.

If you scored 21 - 30, you have *low autonomy* in your relationship and need to love yourself more and practice daily autonomy builders.

AUTONOMY-BUILDERS TO PRACTICE EACH DAY

- Say positive affirmations out loud to claim your value. For example: "I am good enough just the way I am. I have inherent value. My talents and abilities are useful to others. I am loved by my Creator."
- Do not criticize yourself. Be gentle with your thoughts about yourself. Forgive yourself when you make mistakes. Encourage yourself to progress.
- Stand up for yourself if someone is belittling or abusing you. It is your responsibility to teach people how to treat you.
- Get to know yourself. Ask yourself what you like, what you need, what motivates you, what you are interested in doing, and what kind of life you want to create for yourself.
- Take good care of yourself. Eat foods that nourish you. Exercise thirty minutes a day to de-stress. Rest if you are tired. Take timeouts if you are overwhelmed. Participate in spiritual practices, such as prayer, meditation, or reading spiritual books.
- Set healthy boundaries in your relationships. Do not allow others to take advantage of you or use you for their own benefit. Say "no" to demands and requests that are too much for you.
- Make decisions based on your internal moral compass. Do not seek the approval of others. Be true to who you are and what you know is right.
- Set individual daily goals for your growth and development. Example: "Today, I will take time to research information about something I am interested in," "Today, I will set aside time to problem solve something I have been avoiding," or "Today, I will contribute what I know to add value to those around me."

As you increase your sense of individuality, you will be more comfortable expressing your true self, which allows you to have autonomy in your relationship.

CLIENT STORY

Gladys struggled with low self-esteem and autonomy in her relationship. She came to me for counseling after her husband, Victor, had left their twenty-three-year marriage. When I first met Gladys, I asked her about her upbringing. I learned that her biological father was never in her life, her mother had a significant anger problem, and that she was sexually abused as a child. Gladys did not feel loved or accepted and she did not have a sense of belonging in her family.

She was significantly depressed, not just from Victor leaving, but because she had lost herself in her marriage. She said, "I don't even know what my favorite color is anymore. I wasted my life pleasing Victor, hoping he would see that I am a good person." She went on to say that when she was married, she tried to go to school to be a nurse, which was her dream, but her husband threatened to end their marriage because he wanted her home cooking, cleaning, and taking care of their three children.

Gladys was dependent on her husband to meet her financial and emotional needs. She had not worked much outside of the home. When they had financial problems, Victor prompted her to get a temporary job to help with the bills, but that didn't last long.

I asked Gladys about who she was prior to meeting Victor. She said, "I was working at a college and taking typing classes to become an administrative assistant. I liked to go to dances with my friends and enjoyed being outside and exploring new places."

Gladys started to recall that before meeting Victor, she was independent, providing for herself financially, and enjoying a sense of belonging with friends and her college community.

I gave Gladys daily homework to list all the things she had done for herself before meeting Victor. This allowed her to regain confidence in her ability to take care of herself again. She found a job as an administrative assistant two weeks after she started counseling.

I asked her about her support system. She tearfully explained, "My parents lived thousands of miles from us, and Victor would get angry if I spent time with the women in my neighborhood or at church. We would have friends over to our home, but I would be the one doing all the cooking and cleaning, so I didn't really have time to socialize with them."

I asked Gladys if she felt supported by family or friends before she met Victor.

"Oh yes!" she said. "Margaret, Jenny, and I used to get together weekly to go dancing. I met Victor at a dance."

I asked her how long it had been since she went dancing. "Not since I got married," she softly said, looking down at her feet.

I gave Gladys homework to look up dance activities in her community to remind her of the joy and connectedness she used to feel when dancing with friends and before marrying Victor. I also asked her to reach out to some women in her church and neighborhood and invite them to coffee or lunch.

Gladys returned two weeks later to inform me what had happened. "I invited my neighbor Ruth to lunch, but all she wanted to talk about was my husband leaving. It was terrible. I cried in the restaurant and ended up not eating my lunch. I felt like a scorned woman," she said.

"I am so sorry this happened to you Gladys," I stammered. "A good support system actually lifts you up and wants positive things for your future. It doesn't seem that Ruth is able to do this for you right now." I suggested that Gladys look for a group that had similar interests to her own and build a support system. I acknowledged her strengths and abilities and encouraged her to create a future that excited her.

Over the next several weeks, Gladys joined a sewing group and started doing line-dancing on Tuesday nights at a restaurant/lounge fifteen minutes from her home. I could tell her depression was lifting. Gladys told me she also decided to change churches. "It's too hard for me to keep going to the same church that Victor and I attended together for the past fifteen years," she said. "I want a fresh start with the new, more confident me." She smiled.

After about three months, Gladys had a sense of who she truly was. She said, "I definitely don't want to date. I'm still kind of scared of men. I did a lot of work to get myself back and I don't want to lose 'me' again!"

I gave Gladys the list below so she could remain strong and confident in herself if she decided to date in the future.

EFFECTIVE WAYS TO DEVELOP HEALTHY AUTONOMY IN A RELATIONSHIP

1. Love and value yourself every day. Do not judge your imperfections. As you value yourself more, you can identify the value you bring to your relationships.

2. Stand up for what is important to you, even if it is not important to your partner. This will help you gain self-respect.

3. Set boundaries. Let your partner know how you want him/her to interact with you. Explain the consequences if he/she does not treat you with value.

4. Take time to be alone and reflect on your inherent qualities and how you can share them with others to reach your full potential as a human being.

5. Don't compromise your values, goals, and life dreams in order to please your partner.

6. Create your own happiness, so that you can be happy in your relationship.

7. You do not have to agree with your partner on every issue. It is normal to be different and care about different things.

8. You are not obligated to do what your partner wants, and he/she is not obligated to do what you want. Act equally, respectfully, mutually, and collaboratively with each other.

9. Own what matters to you without expecting your partner's approval or acceptance. In the end, you have to answer to God (not people) for your choices.

10. Do not take responsibility for your partner's choices. He/she is an adult and is responsible for his/her own self-care and choices.

11. Encourage and nurture your own growth, well-being, life dreams, and happiness as well as that of your partner.

12. Let your relationship be a safe place to express your true self and encourage your partner to do the same.

A whole, autonomous person can be a valuable partner that enhances their relationship. A person who is not autonomous drains their partner of energy by looking to him/her to feel secure, confident, and adequate.

What kind of partner are you?

COUPLE'S JOURNAL

Answer the following questions separately. Then, share your answers with your partner to identify the level of autonomy in your relationship.

1. Did you feel loved and accepted in your family growing up? Did you feel a sense of belonging? *(Example: My parents/caretakers told me they loved me. I was encouraged to have my own opinions and interests growing up. My parents/caretakers encouraged me to be a part of our family activities.)*

_____

_____

_____

_____

_____

_____

_____

_____

_____

2. How do you love and accept yourself today? *(Example: I value myself by taking good care of my body. I think kind thoughts about myself. I am confident in my abilities. I encourage myself to do what I am interested in.)*

_____

_____

_____

_____

_____

_____

_____

_____

_____

3. What do you do to feel a sense of belonging with your partner or family? *(Example: I spend time with my partner and family on a regular basis. I include my partner or family in my life goals and plans. I tell my partner and family how important they are to me.)*

_____

_____

_____

_____

_____

_____

_____

_____

_____

_____

4. How do you encourage your partner to reach their full potential? *(Example: I encourage my partner to have his/her own friends. I acknowledge my partner's abilities and talents and encourage his/her success. I listen to what is important to my partner without trying to convince him/her of agreeing with my ideas.)*

_____

_____

_____

_____

_____

_____

_____

_____

_____

Ask your partner the following questions and write down his/her answers to enhance autonomy in your relationship.

1. How can I encourage you to be yourself in our relationship? *(Example: listen to your life dreams and support your purpose, encourage you in areas of personal growth, encourage you to pursue what is important to you)*

_____

_____

_____

_____

_____

_____

_____

_____

_____

2. What can I do to strengthen your sense of belonging in our relationship? *(Example: Plan a future together, include you in daily activities with me, tell you that I am glad we are partners together on our life journey)*

_____

_____

_____

_____

_____

_____

_____

_____

_____

COUPLE'S HOMEWORK

Write down the ways your partner has encouraged you to be an autonomous person since you met him/her. Share what you write with each other.

Date:

To: From:

You encouraged me to be and express my true self when…

_____

_____

_____

_____

_____

_____

_____

_____

_____

_____

Date:

To: From:

You encouraged me to be and express my true self when…

_____

_____

_____

_____

_____

_____

_____

_____

_____

_____

Elisabeth Davies, M.C.

LOVE TIP

Tell your partner how he/she can support you deepening and expressing your true self. Thank him/her each time.

INTENTION

We make our relationship
a safe place to fully express
who we are to each other.

AFFIRMATION

When God created
[partner's name],
He intentionally infused him/her
with special gifts and abilities
that make him/her unique
and separate from me and my talents.
I feel blessed to support
[partner's name]
as a partner
in reaching his/her full potential
as a valuable person,
and I receive his/her support
in doing the same for me.

Elisabeth Davies, M.C.

Chapter 10

Romance Enhancers

Read this chapter together as a couple. Take time to discuss your thoughts and suggestions for more romance in your relationship.

Romance can diminish over the years of being together. The routine and responsibilities of everyday life can set in and leave little time or thought for romance with your loved one. Romance takes effort, creativity, and giving of yourself to your partner. When you have been together many years, it is easy to lose the romantic feelings you may have had early on when dating. Romance is crucial if you don't want to feel like just a roommate to your partner.

Romance is the act of showing your love interest for each other. Common romantic gestures can be giving your partner flowers, writing him/her a love note, or doing thoughtful activities that make you feel especially cherished by each other.

If your partner is the romantic type, that is great! If not, then you will also need to contribute ideas and activities that enhance romance, for closeness to ensue. Think about what made you fall in love with your partner in the first place. Remember how you met: recall milestones of the first date, first kiss, first time you held hands, or first time you were intimate with each other. Memories can remind you of how you fell in love in the first place and fuel your motivation to plan romantic moments from this state of mind.

CLIENT STORY

Rebecca and Eric came to counseling when the romance in their marriage was at an all-time low. Rebecca said, "My sister died unexpectedly last year. We were really close. We talked on the phone every week and saw each other often. Since then, I have had no desire to go on dates or be romantic with Eric."

"Have you had any grief counseling or support for your loss?" I asked her.

"I attended Grief Share at my church and had support through my women's group," Rebecca answered. "I also read a really good book that helped me through the loss."

Eric responded, "Rebecca doesn't sit close to me anymore when we watch TV. She doesn't cuddle with me in bed anymore. She is irritated and impatient with me when I try to get close to her."

"I want our relationship to go back to the way it was before my sister died," Rebecca said. "I feel bad that I have no desire to be close with Eric. We have talked about it, but I don't know how to rekindle the romance and desire I once had."

I gave Rebecca and Eric homework to go back and look at their wedding album together and look through pictures and old videos to reminisce about times when the romance and closeness were strong. I suggested they both make note of the activities that enhanced romance in the past.

Two weeks later they came back to their counseling appointment.

"How is everything going?" I asked.

"I have been starting slow," Rebecca responded. "I have been sitting next to Eric more and cuddling in bed. I have been holding his hand when we go for walks. Looking back at old pictures together made me laugh and reminded me of how happy I used to be with Eric."

"That's great, Rebecca," I replied. "When you go through grief or a big loss, it can steal your joy and it is easy to withdraw from activities that were once enjoyable. You must fight for joy every day. Nobody is promised tomorrow. Every morning, ask yourself, 'What am I going to do today that will bring me joy?' Intentionally create these moments each day that impregnate and grow joy in your being. This simple exercise can help you overcome grief, loss, and depression so that you can have a relationship and life that you look forward to each day when you wake up."

Rebecca nodded her head.

Eric said, "I want to be there for you Rebecca. I love you and it hurts me when you are sad. I don't know what to say or how to get close to you when you won't let me in."

"It's not you, Eric," Rebecca said, looking at him. "Losing my sister took away all my motivation. I am just trying to get through each day. I have no energy to give to you or anyone."

I asked her, "What used to bring you joy before your sister died?"

She thought for a moment, and then slowly said, "Dancing, music, learning Spanish, making crafts, and baking chocolate desserts."

"How about you and Eric dance in your living room twice a week for several minutes, or have Eric help you practice your Spanish? Teach him one of your chocolate recipes so you can enjoy being together again," I suggested.

"I would like that," Rebecca smiled.

Two weeks later when Eric and Rebecca arrived for their counseling appointment, they were holding hands. Rebecca sat close to Eric on my couch.

I smiled and said, "I can feel the joy!"

Rebecca laughed. "We are having so much fun dancing two nights a week in our living room, but Eric cannot bake, and he can't pronounce words correctly in Spanish!"

Eric laughed, "We ended up laughing so hard when I was trying to help her with her Spanish! And Rebecca is right, I should really leave all the baking to her."

Eric and Rebecca discovered that doing enjoyable activities together as a couple enhanced the romance in their relationship.

ROMANCE ENHANCERS

- Make or give your partner a special gift that shows how much you love him/her.
- Leave love notes for your partner in his/her car or places he/she will find them.
- Be affectionate often. Hold hands, cuddle, squeeze and caress each other.
- Flirt and be charming. Wink, smile, and say something that softens his/her heart to yours.
- Make your partner's favorite drink or food and tell him/her you were thinking of him/her.
- Give your partner flowers or tickets to his/her favorite event.
- Ask your partner to slow-dance to romantic music with you.
- Invite your partner to run away with you for a few hours.
- Offer to help your partner with a project because you enjoy spending time with him/her.
- Tell your partner what you love most about him/her. Verbalize your love for him/her often.
- Go on a picnic together or take a walk in a beautiful place.
- Plan a romantic getaway together.
- Do a kind act or favor that reduces his/her stress.
- Be gentle and kind with your words.
- Write a romantic poem or song for him/her.

ROMANTIC POEM

After all these years, I can still look at you
and see the beautiful soul I fell in love with.
Your touch still invites chemistry.
Your gaze illuminates your love for me.
The stories you share let me know you still care.
Close we lay at night, silent in our deeply connected hearts, knowing our romance continues through the years.

Sparking the romance in your relationship can be a surprise, or you can plan it and let your partner know the time and date you need him/her to be available for romancing.

Dating is one way to keep romance alive in your relationship. This quality time builds your love together as a couple. When you date, wear something beautiful, smell beautiful, and spend time to look your best for your partner. Intentionally share your best, positive self with him/her. Go places that have an atmosphere that enhances romance, a place with candlelight, romantic music, or relaxing ambiance. Make it fun and memorable.

Dating your partner is a wonderful opportunity to leave the past tensions and worries of the week behind and focus on building more loving feelings with your partner during your romantic time together.

Make time for romance in your relationship at least two to four times each month to nurture your love and feelings of adoration for one another.

COUPLE'S JOURNAL

Answer the following writing prompts and share them with your partner.

1. My first romantic experience with you was …

_____

_____

_____

_____

_____

_____

_____

_____

Elisabeth Davies, M.C.

2. Ask your partner what you can do to keep the romance flowing with him/her *(Example: Write loving messages to him/her, hug and say, "I love you," slow dance together)*

_____
_____
_____
_____
_____
_____
_____
_____
_____
_____

3. What can your partner do to add more romance in your relationship? *(Example: Cuddle more, flirt with you, buy you flowers or gifts)*

_____
_____
_____
_____
_____
_____
_____
_____
_____
_____
_____

4. How often would you like to have a romantic experience with your partner? *(Example: Every day, weekly, every other week)*

_____

_____

_____

COUPLE'S HOMEWORK

Plan a romantic experience with your partner. Write down your plans. *(Example: I'm going to have my partner's favorite meal waiting when he/she gets home from work, I will have candles and rose petals on the table and soft music playing, I will wear something sexy and flirt with him/her while I pour his/her wine)*

_____

_____

_____

_____

_____

_____

_____

_____

_____

_____

_____

_____

_____

_____

_____

_____

_____

_____

Elisabeth Davies, M.C.

LOVE TIP

Leave love notes for your partner to find. This lets him/her know you are thinking of him/her and can spark more romantic feelings.

INTENTION

The romantic feelings in our relationship increase
as I recall all the magnetic moments
that draw me into loving you.

AFFIRMATION

I create romantic moments with
[partner's name]
that make him/her smile
because I let [partner's name]
know how much I enjoy being close
and cherishing the love I have for him/her.

Elisabeth Davies, M.C.

Chapter 11

More Intimacy and Passion

Read this chapter together as a couple. Take time to discuss your thoughts and suggestions on intimacy and passion.

For your relationship to be gratifying, intimacy and passion must be part of it. This includes sexual desire, lust, excitement, new experiences, anticipation, thrill, and delight. Passion is what keeps you interested, attracted, and wanting more time with your partner.

Passion typically lasts between two to three years in a committed relationship.[iv] This means you will have to bring new ideas and activities into play if you have been together after this point.

You may think it is your partner's responsibility to sexually pursue you, romance you, and bring ideas that infuse passion into your relationship. If your partner thinks that this is his/her sole responsibility, lucky you! If not, then you need to share in this effort so that both of you are contributing and receiving desirous ideas and activities that keep the intimacy and attraction strong.

I have counseled thousands of couples over the past twenty-seven years. In my experience, most often, the man will complain there is a lack of affection in the relationship, while the woman will complain she does not feel emotionally supported by her partner. Research shows men have a higher libido and therefore think about sex and desire it more often than women, whereas most women prefer to talk, connect, and then have sex with their partner. For a man, sex is the connection in the relationship.[v]

A lack of sex or affection in your relationship is often caused by some type of disconnect with your partner. The disconnect usually stems from one of the five foundations being damaged: communication, commitment, respect, trust, or love in the relationship. Even if your relationship is strong in all five areas, it can still take quite a bit of vulnerability on your part to keep passion and intimacy flowing with your partner.

IDEAS TO KEEP THE PASSION STRONG

- Write down what turns you on and share this with your partner. Incorporate this into your lovemaking.
- Ask your partner what turns him/her on. Incorporate this into your lovemaking.
- Leave sexy notes in your partners car or places that he/she will find them.
- Tell your partner what you find most attractive about him/her.
- Buy something that you think will look sexy on your partner and give it to him/her.
- Wear something sexy when you are with your partner. Flirt with him/her.
- Take your partner somewhere neither of you have ever been and make out with him/her.
- Be affectionate with your partner often.
- Write a sexy song about your partner and sing it to him/her (if you have the ability).
- Write a sexy poem or story for your partner (if you have the ability) and read it to him/her.
- Invite your partner to take a bubble bath or shower with you.
- Watch a sexy movie together.

If your partner and you have children, jobs, and responsibilities like many couples, you may have to plan dates away from this to allow for more intimacy and passion together. Children, the phone ringing, pressure from responsibilities, and fatigue can all kill the mood for intimacy.

CLIENT STORY

Intimacy was difficult for Laura, a thirty-three-year-old mother of two boys. She came to me for counseling because she said sex with her husband, Jason, was painful, and she did not enjoy it. She went on to say she was exhausted from working full time and having to care for their nine-year-old son who had juvenile diabetes.

I worked with Laura on better self-care to minimize her fatigue. I suggested she take at least thirty minutes each day to recharge her energy by doing what she enjoys. I explained that the better she takes care of herself, the more energy she will have to give her husband, children, and work. I also suggested she let her gynecologist know about her pain during intercourse.

During our session, I asked Laura to tell me the first thoughts that came to her mind when I asked her to finish the sentence, "Sex is…"

She responded, "Painful, uncomfortable." She hesitated and then said, "I wish I didn't feel this way."

"How do you want sex with Jason to be?" I asked.

"Enjoyable, like I don't dread it or feel guilty if I don't have sex with him," she answered.

"What would have to be different so you could enjoy sex with Jason?" I enquired.

"Feeling better about my body. Maybe time away with Jason, no kids, no work, no worrying about our son."

"Can you plan a night or weekend where you and Jason could do that? Planning dates with him shows that romance and time to connect is important to you. This will also give you an opportunity to set the mood for intimacy," I recommended.

Laura signed up for my women's body image group. She learned new ways to appreciate and take care of her body. Laura started exercising three days a week for thirty minutes at a time. She became more conscious of eating whole foods that gave her more energy. She also practiced loving body affirmations that helped her stop being so critical of her weight. She started to feel better about her body because she was intentionally taking better care of it. Taking good care of your physical health will increase your body image, even when you are not at your ideal weight.

Laura came back to individual counseling three weeks later.

"How is intimacy with Jason now?" I asked.

"Better," Laura smiled. "My mom and dad babysat the boys overnight last weekend. Jason and I stayed home. It was so nice to have the house to ourselves. We took a shower together and gave each other naked massages."

"Wonderful!" I cheered. "I would like you to plan dates with Jason two to four times every month so that you can keep the intimacy and passion between you flowing."

For women to enjoy intimacy, it often requires energy, connection with their partner, and foreplay. For men, having sex can be a stress relief, and it often does not take much time to get them in the mood.

It is important that both partners want to have sex and are not just going through the motions without real desire. This is where setting the mood can make a big difference.

TIPS FOR SETTING THE MOOD FOR INTIMACY

- No kids around (or at least not awake).
- A relaxed mind (no worries or to-do lists going through your mind).
- No distractions or devices that take your attention away from being present with your partner.
- A calm environment for focusing (quiet or soft noise).
- Privacy for freedom to be intimate.
- Openness to affection, closeness, and vulnerability.
- Free of past resentments, anger, and hurts toward your partner.
- Healthy body image (feel physically attractive).
- Good hygiene, free of off-putting odors.

COUPLE'S JOURNAL

Answer the following questions and share them with your partner.

1. What stimulates your desire for your partner? *(Example: Him/Her reading sexy stories to you, sharing secret desires, foreplay)*

_____

_____

_____

_____

_____

_____

_____

_____

_____

_____

_____

2. Ask your partner what stimulates his/her desire for you? *(Example: Dancing together, cooking naked together, a massage from you)*

_____

_____

_____

_____

_____

_____

_____

_____

_____

_____

_____

3. What do you find most attractive about your partner? *(Example: His/Her legs, his/her eyes, his/her smile)*

_____

_____

_____

_____

_____

_____

_____

_____

_____

_____

_____

4. Ask your partner what they find most attractive about you *(Example: Your body, your hugs, your kisses)*

_____

_____

_____

_____

_____

_____

_____

_____

_____

_____

_____

_____

5. What can you do to keep passion and intimacy flowing in your relationship? *(Example: Show more affection, leave love notes for your partner, plan new things to do as a couple)*

_____

_____

_____

_____

_____

_____

_____

_____

_____

_____

_____

_____

6. What can your partner do to keep passion and intimacy flowing in your relationship? (*Example: He/She can be more flirtatious, initiate more sex, kiss you more*)

_____

_____

_____

_____

_____

_____

_____

_____

_____

_____

_____

COUPLE'S HOMEWORK

Each of you, do at least one activity this week that amps up the passion in your relationship. You can use ideas off the list in this chapter or your own to enhance passion with your partner. Write down what you will do.

1. To amp up the passion in my relationship, I will…

_____

_____

_____

_____

_____

_____

_____

_____

2. To amp up the passion in my relationship, I will…

_____

_____

_____

_____

_____

_____

_____

LOVE TIP

Share sexual fantasies with each other. This can help your partner become a better lover to you.

INTENTION

The passion in our relationship grows
as I initiate affection, romantic moments,
and plan for shared excitement.

AFFIRMATION

I choose to see the good in
[partner's name]
each day and connect in ways
that deepen our passion.

*

122

Chapter 12

Building A Deep Friendship with Your Partner

Read this chapter together as a couple. Take time to discuss your thoughts and suggestions on friendship.

If I were to sum up two important qualities in a monogamous partner, they would be good friend and lover because those qualities make time spent together more enjoyable for years.

There are several traits that make you a good friend. Loyalty is one. Not bad-mouthing your partner or doing things that make him/her feel you are not on their team is another. Being a good listener, caring, and being supportive are also good friend traits. It is important when building a deep friendship with your partner that you refrain from judging or condemning. It is fine to give constructive criticism that helps him/her grow, but do not accuse or make comments that tear down his/her self-esteem. Look for the good qualities in your partner, even if he/she is having a bad day. A good friend is honest with you, trustworthy, and dependable. You can count on him/her to keep promises and follow through with the plans he/she makes with you. A good friend is positive and fun to be around. He/she is not a chronic complainer when it comes to doing activities with you.

It takes a lot of skill to be a good friend. These are skills you can practice and learn to master over time. Know that you and your partner will go through many new and difficult situations over the years, so it is not realistic to think you can be a good friend or partner all the time. However, if you practice on a consistent basis, you will have a more gratifying time together.

Think about the friendships you currently have and reflect on the qualities that keep you enjoying those friendships.

CLIENT STORY

I remember what great friends Brock and Kendall were. They came to me for couple's counseling after they both got laid off from their jobs at the same time. They met each other working at a restaurant that had recently closed.

They were not sure if they should move back to Colorado (near their parents who would provide more support with their one-year-old) or stay in Arizona and start their own business or look for a new career altogether.

They had been married for five years before having their daughter. Kendall had anxiety about their finances and future. She was a planner. Brock was a go-with-the-flow, "everything is going to work out" kind of a guy.

When I asked him what some of his ideas were regarding a career, he said, "Kendall and I work really well together. We are a good team and we both enjoy cooking together. I think we should start our own virtual cooking show online and get restaurants to fund it by recommending our viewers eat at their establishments."

I asked Brock if he had ever been self-employed before.

"No, but I have been a cook for over ten years and worked in the restaurant industry for fourteen years. I know we could do it," he confidently said.

I asked Kendall what she thought.

"It's really risky. There are no guarantees it will work out, and we have a baby to support."

"You already know so many people in the restaurant industry," Brock said, looking at Kendall. "They love you. All we have to do is record a couple of episodes of us cooking and show the owners and ask for their support. You know they would do it."

I encouraged them to try it out and for Kendall to have a backup plan if it made her more at ease.

Two weeks later, Brock and Kendall came back to counseling and showed me a video they had made of them cooking. They were having so much fun!

As I watched them on the screen, I could see they were a great team. Kendall was prepping the ingredients and explaining what she was doing while Brock was heating up the pan and sharing the appropriate temperature for the meal. They were joking around about a mistake they had made in the past by adding too much pepper to the recipe. It was obvious they were having a wonderful time, like great friends in a kitchen enjoying the same activity. At the end of the video, they told their viewers if they didn't want to cook this meal at home, "Louis's restaurant has this dish on their menu, and it's as delicious as ours!"

I said, "This is a great video. I enjoyed the cooking tips and watching you two together makes me smile."

Kendall said, "We showed the video to the owner of Louis's restaurant, and he asked us to make him a video he can play on the TV screen in his farm-to-table restaurant to encourage his customers to buy local ingredients."

"That's great!" I responded, "And now you're in business!"

Even though Brock and Kendall experienced stress in their marriage when they were laid off, their friendship and team camaraderie helped them create something good together.

To be a good friend to your partner, you must be a good friend to yourself. Remember, what is on the inside of you (your thoughts, feelings, and beliefs) get projected out in your relationships.

WAYS TO DEEPEN
YOUR BOND OF FRIENDSHIP

- Practice being nonjudgmental, caring, and supportive of each other's needs. Ask your partner, "What do you need from me?" or "How can I support you today?"
- Forgive yourself and your partner for his/her imperfections. Offer grace and mercy for mistakes and shortcomings. This will allow you to get along better and have more freedom to be authentic with each other.
- Accept that you have good in you, even if you are not having a good day or make a poor choice. This allows you to see the good in your partner more often and strengthen a loving friendship.
- Practice keeping the promises you make by following through on what you say you are going to do. This builds trust, shows dependability, and boosts confidence in one another.
- Look for opportunities to have fun: dance together, sing, paint, play, or do something you both really enjoy.
- Spend time getting to know each other. Find out what motivates him/her. What are his/her likes and dislikes? Stay curious so you can be better at helping each other.
- Build a habit of positive internal dialogue and daily gratitude to enhance your mood and share positive moods and words with each other.

EXAMPLES OF POSITIVE INTERNAL DIALOGUE

- I am a unique and valuable human being.
- I deserve to be loved by myself and others.
- There is a purpose and meaning to my life.
- My best is always good enough.
- The better I am to me, the better I can be to others.
- I do not need to prove my worth or inherent value to anyone.

FRIEND POEM

I'll be a friend to you when times are good or bad.
I'll be a friend to you when you're happy or sad,
Because a good friend knows that true friendship lasts
through all life's woes.
I'll lift you up when you feel down.
I'll comfort you when no one is around.
To you, I will always be true,
Because friendship is a gift,
one that I will always cherish.
One that in my mind will never perish.

COUPLE'S JOURNAL

Answer the following questions individually, then share them with your partner.

1. What do you say or do that proves you are a good friend to yourself? *(Example: I do not criticize myself when I make mistakes. I encourage myself when I do difficult things. I listen to my needs and meet them.)*

_____

_____

_____

_____

_____

2. In what ways is your partner a good friend to you? *(Example: He/she is trustworthy, loyal, caring)*

_____

_____

_____

_____

_____

_____

_____

_____

3. Ask your partner, "How can I be a better friend to you?" What did he/she say?

_____

_____

_____

_____

_____

_____

_____

_____

4. What friendship qualities would you like to enhance in your relationship? *(Example: Better listening, fewer negative comments, have more fun together)*

_____

_____

_____

_____

_____

_____

_____

_____

COUPLE'S HOMEWORK

Write down what you will do each week to deepen the friendship with your partner. *(Example: Point out my partner's good qualities, do an unexpected kind favor for my partner, ask my partner how I can be more supportive)*

1. This week, I will …

_____

_____

_____

_____

_____

_____

_____

_____

_____

_____

_____

2. This week, I will …

_____

_____

_____

_____

_____

_____

_____

_____

_____

_____

_____

_____

Elisabeth Davies, M.C.

LOVE TIP

Invite your partner to do enjoyable activities with you, such as a playdate, games, or events that deepen friendship.

INTENTION

I am mindful of creating friendly interactions with my partner
so we can build a lasting friendship together.

AFFIRMATION

I choose to see the good in
[partner's name]
each day and connect in ways
that deepen our friendship.

Elisabeth Davies, M.C.

Chapter 13

Time for Adventure and Fun

Read this chapter together as a couple. Take time to discuss your thoughts and suggestions for more fun and adventure.

In addition to engaging in experiences together that build deep friendship, it is essential to incorporate adventure and fun so that your relationship does not become monotonous.

Adventure means doing something unusual, exciting, or new; exploring unknown territory. It does not have to be expensive or be far from home. Adventure is about exposing yourself to amusing, exhilarating experiences. They can even be unexpected or risky. These kinds of experiences as a couple interrupt the day-to-day routine that is easy to fall into when you have been together for many years. Sharing fun activities gives you both something to talk about and enjoy together.

Do not wait for your partner to plan an adventure for you. If you want adventure in your relationship, share your ideas and invite your partner to join you. If your partner declines your invitation, express why you would enjoy more adventures together as a couple. Ask your partner for ideas too.

Every day of living can be an adventure because something unexpected happens each day—you just have to pay attention. This could be meeting new people, engaging in conversations you have never had, or gazing at scenery you have not seen. Look for the different in each day and plan for adventure with your partner so that your relationship does not get boring, and you do not lose interest in spending time together.

My husband and I had a terrific adventure that started in April 2017 and lasted until October 2018. When we became empty-nesters, we moved out of our home, bought a used RV, and traveled to thirty-five states across America, two provinces in Canada, and two states in Mexico. We traveled over 20,000 miles! My husband and I are both self-employed, so we were able to work as we traveled. It was one of the best adventures we have ever had in the twenty-seven years we have been married. We created new memories that we still talk about today. It enhanced our closeness because we had to be a tight team when we were traveling. I would help find RV parks for overnight parking and map out the roads and freeways while my husband drove and managed the mechanics of our RV. This adventure took away the mundane routine of daily living and infused newness; something to look forward to each day.

IDEAS FOR ADDING ADVENTURE INTO YOUR RELATIONSHIP

- Go on a trip. Visit a place you have never been.
- Come up with objects to find in your community and go on a local treasure hunt together.
- Explore a cave or underwater cavern.
- Go sky diving.
- Go on an ultra-light aviation flight.
- Go river rafting, canoeing, or kayaking.
- Take a cooking class or a dance class.
- Do an escape room experience.
- Hike a new canyon or mountain.
- Go snorkeling or scuba diving.
- Build something together, such as a doghouse, bird feeder, home project, etc.
- Visit a museum or art gallery.
- Pack a picnic and visit a new park or nature site.
- Do something new that you are both curious about.

FUN POEM

Fun is something all can have, who are in favor.
Explore the "new" and make life an experience to savor.
Bring your partner along for a new, titillating adventure,
one you will revel in and chalk up together as a life-quencher!

There will be times in your relationship when it is difficult to plan for fun and adventure together. Maybe one of you is experiencing grief, loss, or depression. Illness, financial stress, frequent arguments, or unresolved hurts all make it harder to enjoy activities together as a couple. It is important that no matter what season or life situation you are in, you intentionally practice thoughts of gratitude and do activities that bring you joy. This opens a life sprinkled with adventure and fun.

CLIENT STORY

Jack and Renee were experiencing difficult times that made it hard to plan for adventure in their marriage. They came to me for counseling after being married forty-five years. Jack was recently retired, but Renee was still working. Their four children were grown. Their thirty-six-year-old daughter, Samantha, and her two children had recently moved in with them following Samantha's divorce. Jack started to have heart problems; he felt stress from the added responsibility of taking care of his grandchildren while Samantha was at work. Renee was concerned with the decline in Jack's health. Plus, she was exhausted from her full-time job and having added expenses from her daughter and grandchildren.

I asked what they were doing for self-care and fun to de-stress. Jack admitted he was not setting good boundaries with his daughter. He was taking his grandchildren to school during the week and cooking dinner every night. He said, "I have been picking up these responsibilities because Samantha is depressed, and when she gets home from work she goes straight to the bedroom and cries from her divorce. I feel bad for the kids because she is not taking care of them."

"It is good to help our family and loved ones, but not at the expense of our own mental health, physical health, and financial stability. How can you help your daughter and grandchildren without compromising your health and finances?" I asked Jack.

Jack didn't have an answer.

Renee looked at him and said, "Your doctor already told you your blood pressure is too high and that your heart cannot handle the stress. Samantha made selfish choices that led to her divorce, and she is not thinking about her children right now either. Her selfishness is affecting your health and our marriage, and this is why we are at the counselor's office when Samantha should be in counseling, not us!"

"Wow, Renee!" I laughed, and turned to Jack. "Do you think there is truth in what Renee is saying? Could you be enabling Samantha by not giving her full responsibility to take care of her own children when she is not at work?"

"I hate to see my grandchildren not taken care of." Jack said, tearfully. "This whole situation breaks my heart."

"We raised our kids. It is not our responsibility to raise our grandchildren, too," Renee emphasized.

"Renee has a very good point," I responded. "Can the children's father take them until Samantha is able to take better care of them?"

"He works full-time and is a sports coach after work. He is hardly ever home." Renee commented.

After three sessions and many suggestions, Jack and Renee agreed to have a talk with their ex-son-in-law about taking his children every other weekend. They also asked their three sons if they could help with their niece and nephew to allow Jack and Renee to get away each weekend to de-stress and rebuild Jack's health by having fun with new adventures together. They also gave their daughter a three-month deadline to find another place to live.

Two months later, Jack and Renee came back to counseling for a follow-up visit. Jack reported less stress and better health due to the fun adventures he and Renee were having on their weekends together.

"Jack has been planning surprise weekend getaways for us while I am at work," Renee smiled. "Each Friday when I get off work, he has my bag packed, waiting for me. It has added so much adventure and fun to our marriage!"

I asked how Samantha was doing.

"Samantha told us she couldn't afford to move out of our home, so Jack and I decided to put our house up for sale," Renee announced. "This is the only permanent solution to having our daughter not live with us. We are moving to a smaller home in a retirement community where residents must be fifty-five years or older to live there. We are both looking forward to this move. Our three sons are helping us pack and our grandchildren are spending more time with their father now."

"How did Samantha react when you told her?" I asked.

"She was angry," Jack responded. "But she is already dating someone and says she can live with him when we move."

There are always solutions to stressful life situations. In Jack and Renee's situation, part of the solution was declining to take on extra responsibility they could not handle and making more time to do enjoyable activities together.

COUPLE 'S JOURNAL

Answer the following questions individually. Then share them with your partner.

1. What adventures have you and your partner enjoyed together? *(Example: gone on a trip, hiked a canyon, kayaked)*

_____

_____

_____

_____

_____

_____

_____

_____

_____

_____

_____

_____

2. What new adventures would you enjoy with your partner? *(Example: exploring an underground cavern, scuba diving, learning a foreign language together)*

_____

_____

_____

_____

_____

_____

_____

_____

_____

_____

_____

_____

3. Ask your partner what new adventure he/she would enjoy with you. Write down what he/she says.

_____

_____

_____

_____

_____

_____

_____

_____

_____

_____

4. How often would you like to have a fun adventure with your partner? *(Example: once a week, monthly, twice a year)*

_____

_____

_____

_____

_____

_____

_____

_____

_____

_____

_____

_____

_____

5. How do you think having more fun and adventure with your partner will enhance your relationship? *(Example: It will mitigate our mundane routine, it will infuse our relationship with more enjoyable memories, it will de-stress our life)*

_____
_____
_____
_____
_____
_____
_____
_____
_____
_____
_____
_____
_____
_____
_____
_____
_____
_____
_____
_____
_____
_____
_____
_____
_____
_____

COUPLE'S HOMEWORK

Plan a fun adventure with your partner. Write down what you will do and when you will do it.

_____

_____

_____

_____

_____

_____

_____

_____

_____

_____

_____

_____

_____

_____

_____

_____

_____

_____

_____

_____

_____

_____

_____

_____

_____

_____

_____

Elisabeth Davies, M.C.

LOVE TIP

Invite your partner to do enjoyable activities with you. Plan visiting and experiencing new places, listening to new music, learning new games, or doing things that enhance fun and adventure in your relationship.

INTENTION

I invite opportunities to have fun
and make our life together more adventurous
through laughing, playing,
and experiencing new activities.

AFFIRMATION

I initiate more fun experiences
and enjoyable activities with
[partner's name].

Elisabeth Davies, M.C.

Chapter 14

Being Happy in Your Relationship

Read this chapter together as a couple. Take time to discuss your thoughts and suggestions on being happy.

If you and your partner have been together many years, you probably have experienced loss, adversity, and challenging times that may have robbed your happiness. Hardships are a part of life. It is important to intentionally seek joyful experiences so that discouragement and letdowns do not snowball into misery and unhappiness in your relationship.

Happiness is a mental, emotional state of well-being created by satisfaction and meaning in your life. It is your ability to feel positive emotions as well as your capacity to recover quickly from negative emotions. Happiness grows from your contented thinking and enjoying life's natural pleasures like good food, beautiful sunsets, oceans, stars, animals, and people. Decades of research and studies show that people who say they are happy have strong connections with other people and their community.[vi]

For years, I had a magnet on my refrigerator that said this:

> If you really want to be happy, nobody can stop you.

What a great reminder! I looked at it daily to be mindful of this truth.

As crazy as it sounds, not everybody wants to be happy. I have met hundreds of clients and numerous peers who are committed to misery. They chronically complain. They lack gratitude. They look for what is wrong rather than what is right in people and situations. The outcome is negative relationships. Pessimism is toxic to our mental and physical health. People who view life through a negative lens experience more depression, anxiety, coronary artery disease, sickness, and have a shorter life expectancy than optimists.[vii]

Well-being is our natural state. This gets overshadowed, however, if we have chosen to ruminate and focus on past negative experiences in our day-to-day life. Negative thoughts impede our ability to be fully present and content, robbing us of happiness and joy.

CLIENT STORY

Lorinda was a pessimist whose psychiatrist referred her to counseling due to her depression. She was overweight, on disability insurance from her job, and was feeling unloved by her husband, who had a terminal illness.

She told me, "I used to be the happy one at work and home. My husband's illness and my son's behavior problems at school got to be too much for me. I lay on the couch all day. I overeat, I'm having thoughts of suicide, and my husband doesn't even care that we are going to lose our home this year if I don't get back to work."

"I'm so sorry about all you are going through, Lorinda. I can see how all of this could take a toll," I said. "Who is your support system?"

"My two girlfriends don't even call me anymore," she said, looking at her feet. "They probably got tired of me complaining."

"How much compassion do you have for yourself going through these difficulties?" I asked.

"I'm too depressed to care," Lorinda trailed off.

I suggested she tell herself compassionate statements every day, like, "I'm sorry you don't feel loved by your husband; you are such a lovable woman," and "I'm sorry your son is having so many behavior problems; he must be hurting about his dad and me and doesn't know how to express his pain in healthy ways."

Lorinda started to sob.

I waited until she cried out her pain.

"I have never talked to myself that way," she sniffed.

"Don't you think that when life is kicking our butt, that is when we need even more love, support, and problem-solving tactics?" I asked.

She chuckled, "Makes sense."

"You will recover from these current adversities and losses so much quicker when you play on your team," I confidently said. "You need hope. You need to know you are loved. You need encouragement and strategies to overcome this!"

Lorinda took a big breath and let out an audible sigh.

I smiled at her, "You came to the right place. You have an optimist as a counselor!"

She smiled back, "That's good, I think."

It took weekly visits for three months before Lorinda was back to work part-time.

I gave her self-esteem homework to increase her self-image through positive self-talk. I had her write a gratitude list every day to counter her depression. I had her do at least three things every day that made her laugh to evoke more joy from within. I had her journal her thoughts and feelings to release negativity and I encouraged her to walk outside twenty minutes each day to release serotonin in her brain from exposure to sunlight. I encouraged her to reach out to her friends and be intentional about not being negative while she was with them.

On month four, Lorinda still did not feel loved by her husband. She learned in counseling that her husband does not get to decide her lovability; she and God do. Her husband still had a terminal illness, but she learned she does not have control over his health, only how she wants to think and feel about it. Her son's behavior improved because she invited him to go on walks with her and to talk about his dad's terminal illness. Her relationship with her girlfriends became better as they spent more positive time together.

Lorinda said, "I am happier because I learned how to like myself and take better care of myself even though my husband hasn't changed."

Love, support, encouragement, and a healthy lifestyle of exercise and good self-care help overcome adversity and combat depression and pessimism.

You can experience happiness by building positive daily habits of gratitude, positive affirmations, and looking for the good in yourself and others. Although happiness comes from your thoughts and beliefs, not from external circumstances, your moods affect the people you live with and are close to. If you are in a relationship with someone who is negative, you can still be happy, because your partner is not in control of your thoughts and moods, you are! Choosing to be a happy person is a gift you give to yourself that overflows to your relationship.

SOME ACTIVITIES THAT EVOKE HAPPINESS AND HELP CREATE HAPPY MEMORIES WITH YOUR PARTNER

- Think back on times when you laughed together, had fun, and really enjoyed each other's company.
- Play cards, board games, or sports together.
- Dance together.
- Listen to uplifting music or sing together.

- Go to sporting events or concerts together.
- Celebrate a meaningful occasion together.
- Watch a comedy together.
- Share funny stories and jokes with each other.
- Connect with each other and friends.
- Cooperate with each other and look for the good in your partner.
- Be silly together.
- Decide to let go of negative past experiences that rob you of happiness.
- Give yourself something to look forward to each day.
- Do a daily gratitude list and look for the good in yourself and your life.

COUPLE'S JOURNAL

Answer the following questions and share them with your partner.

1. Think back on times when you both experienced happy, joy-filled activities together. Write down some of these memories.

_____

_____

_____

_____

_____

_____

_____

_____

_____

_____

_____

_____

_____

_____

_____

_____

    Elisabeth Davies, M.C.

2. When was the last time you did something together that evoked joy or made you laugh? *(Example: Played in the park with your dog, danced together, played a game that made you laugh)*

_____

_____

_____

_____

_____

_____

_____

_____

_____

_____

_____

3. What do you do that makes you feel happy? *(Example: Listen to uplifting music, hang out with friends, play and be silly)*

_____

_____

_____

_____

_____

_____

_____

_____

_____

_____

_____

_____

4. What do you do that evokes happiness in your relationship? *(Example: Have sex, go on fun dates, tell my partner funny jokes)*

_____

_____

_____

_____

_____

_____

_____

_____

_____

_____

_____

5. What does your partner do that contributes to your happiness? *(Example: Threw a surprise party in your honor, paid off one of your debts, gave you something you really needed or wanted)*

_____

_____

_____

_____

_____

_____

_____

_____

_____

_____

_____

Joy is good medicine for your heart!

COUPLE'S HOMEWORK

Ask your partner how you can bring more happiness into their life and write down his/her response. Do at least one of the activities they mentioned each week to create a happier relationship.

LOVE TIP

Practice being in a positive mood and seeking positive interactions with your partner. Let your partner know the happy moments he/she brings to your life.

INTENTION

I am mindful of focusing on positive thoughts
so I can manage my moods
and be happy in my relationship.

AFFIRMATION

Each day, I notice the good in my life
and participate in activities that enhance joy.
Creating happy memories is my daily practice.

Elisabeth Davies, M.C.

Chapter 15

Making Your Relationship a Priority

Read this chapter together as a couple. Take time to discuss your thoughts and suggestions on making your relationship a priority.

Do you remember when you first fell in love with your partner? You looked forward to spending time with him/her. You did not have to work hard at romance or closeness. Fast forward ten or twenty years. How do you still stay in love through challenges like raising children, increased responsibilities, hardships with family, financial stress, health problems, work, and aging?

How do people stay happily married for more than fifty years? What tips do they practice to keep their relationship fulfilling?

Making your relationship a daily priority is a solid start. For anything to grow and thrive, you must put time and energy into it, including your relationship. It must be nurtured to stay healthy. I have counseled many couples who have made other things a priority, causing their relationship to fail.

CLIENT STORY

Jana and Chance came to me for marriage counseling because Chance was not making Jana a priority. He worked two jobs, which took up seventy hours of his time each week. When he was home, he was exhausted and had no energy to give to Jana.

When I asked Chance if it was financially necessary to work two jobs, he said, "Yes, because Jana only works part-time, and we have a big house payment and three kids to support."

Jana disagreed, "I told you before, I don't need a big house. I need you, and the kids need you to be with us!"

I asked Chance, "What do you think the solution is?"

"I think things are fine the way they are. We have a nice home. Our kids have everything they need. I'm tired of Jana criticizing me when I'm just trying to take care of our family."

I asked Chance if he thought Jana, or his children, needed his time to have a close relationship with him.

"My dad worked a lot when I was growing up and I'm fine," he said.

"Did you want time with your dad when you were growing up?" I asked.

"Yes, but he had to work," Chance responded.

"How is your relationship with your dad today?" I inquired.

"He's dead. He died of a heart attack just before my oldest daughter was born," Chance trailed off as he looked down at his shoes.

"I'm sorry to hear that, and I'm sorry he wasn't able to know your children," I replied. "Giving people our time lets them know that they are important to us. Did you feel important to your dad?"

"Sure," Chance shrugged.

Jana joined the conversation. "You told me your dad never told you he loved you. He left our wedding early because he said he had to go meet a client! Don't you remember how mad you were? He never had time for you, and you never have time for us! We are not your priority, and I'm tired of hearing you say, 'Of course you and the kids are a priority, that's why I work so hard to give you everything.'"

Chance shook his head and looked at me as if he wanted me to respond to Jana. I looked at him and motioned for him to respond to his wife.

"It's really hard to come home to you and the kids when you are always complaining that I missed Jake's basketball practice again. I missed Emily's choir performance at school. You say Bart always asks you, 'When is daddy coming home?' You make me feel like an inadequate father and I can never please you. I would rather be at work where I am respected and appreciated."

"Just forget it!" Jana started to cry. "I'm tired of trying to make you be with me and your children. I have begged you for nine years and it has never changed. You would rather be married to your job than me. You would rather be at work than watch your son play basketball. You don't even care that your daughter is an incredible singer, and Bart misses you. I'm so stupid to think you care!"

Jana got up from her chair and looked at me and said, "I'm sorry I wasted your time hoping that marriage counseling would work," and she left my office.

Chance sat for a moment and looked at me and said, "I guess it's over."

I responded, "Chance, your wife and children need you to be an available husband and father. Is this what you want?"

"It's too hard," he said. "I can never make them happy."

"Well, there are solutions if you change your mind," I reassured him. "Your family is more important than working two jobs to have a big house. I'm sorry your father didn't role model that for you, but I'm even more sorry you are willing to lose your family rather than give the people who love you your time."

Chance thanked me and left to go back to work.

Many people struggle to give themselves to a healthy relationship that requires closeness and connection. This is true of anyone who has an unhealthy dependency/addiction. Whether an addiction is to a substance or habit, it is used to avoid connecting to one's authentic self, making it impossible to have close relationships with others. Chance may have been a workaholic to distract him from being present with connecting to his family.

Giving your partner time each day proves that your relationship is important to you. It also shows your partner that it is important to you to keep the relationship close and connected.

TIPS FOR MAKING YOUR RELATIONSHIP A PRIORITY

- Tell your partner how important it is to you to have a good relationship with him/her.
- Listen to your partner and practice doing what you know is important to him/her so he/she does not have to remind you over and over.
- Ask your partner on a date once a week.
- Ask your partner his/her opinion so that he/she knows you value his/her thoughts and feelings.
- When you argue, ask your partner what you can do to resolve problems and work together in harmony.
- Invite your partner with you when you go to the store or run errands so you can spend more time together.
- Ask your partner what he/she needs from you, so he/she knows you are considerate of being a good partner and making your relationship a priority.
- Be affectionate so your partner knows you value closeness in your relationship.
- Ask your partner how you can help with chores or responsibilities to take stress off of him/her.

- Do random acts of kindness for your partner so he/she knows you care.
- Check in with your partner every day. Ask him/her how their day went.

COUPLE'S JOURNAL

Answer the following questions. Share them with your partner.

1. Ask your partner how much time he/she needs from you to feel important and know you prioritize your relationship. Write down what he/she says.

_____

_____

_____

_____

_____

_____

_____

_____

_____

_____

2. How do you make your relationship a priority each day? *(Example: I call my partner when I am at work. I listen to him/her tell me about his/her day. I am fully present when my partner is talking to me, without being distracted by the cell phone, TV, or internet.)*

_____

_____

_____

_____

_____

_____

_____

_____

_____

3. What does your partner do or say that makes you feel you are a priority to him/her? (*Example: He/She asks to spend time with me, he/she brings me coffee each morning, he/she asks what I need when he/she goes to the store*)

_____

_____

_____

_____

_____

_____

_____

_____

_____

_____

4. How can you give your partner more attention? (*Example: Have meals together, date more often, offer to help him/her with a project or chores*)

_____

_____

_____

_____

_____

_____

_____

_____

_____

_____

_____

_____

COUPLE'S HOMEWORK

Set aside at least ten minutes every day to give your partner your attention. Write down what you did each day for one week.

_____

_____

_____

_____

_____

_____

_____

_____

_____

_____

_____

_____

_____

_____

_____

_____

_____

_____

_____

_____

_____

_____

_____

_____

_____

_____

_____

_____

_____

LOVE TIP

Spend time being present with your partner without distractions. Get to know what he/she likes. Listen to him/her share life plans and ways to grow together as a couple.

INTENTION

I make time each day for my relationship,
so my partner knows he/she is a priority to me.

AFFIRMATION

Our relationship is a gift
I choose to cultivate by giving
[partner's name] the best of myself.
I value [partner's name]
and make him/her a priority in my life.

The sign on the easel reads:

TONIGHT

COUPLES

YOGA

Elisabeth Davies, M.C.

Chapter 16

Becoming Less Self-Centered and More Relationship-Centered

Read this chapter together as a couple. Take time to discuss your thoughts and suggestions on becoming more relationship centered.

When you go from being single to being in a relationship that is important to you, you must learn to be less self-centered and more relationship-centered for your partnership to be healthy and thrive.

"Relationship-centered" means you are cognizant of making decisions that benefit the relationship, not just yourself. You are intentional about giving what you can to enhance the relationship. Being self-centered in a relationship means you are in it with the thought of how it can benefit you. Your needs and wants supersede your partner's and you argue to get your way. Both people must give of themselves and their abilities to strengthen the relationship. This means being a team player and supporting your partner with his/her goals, especially ones that enhance the relationship financially, sexually, emotionally, and spiritually.

It is easy to think about what you need from your relationship and not be mindful of your partner's needs. Both of your needs must be met for the relationship to succeed. It is not about keeping score. Detrimental attitudes like "You meet my needs, then I will meet yours, or you are not meeting my needs, so I won't meet yours," cause division, resentment, and distance in the relationship.

CLIENT STORY

Phoebe and Mark came to me for couple's counseling because they both kept score with each other. During the first session, Mark said, "I'm only agreeing to come to counseling because Phoebe said she would pay if I went."

"Well, since you are here, what would you like to get from our time together, Mark?" I asked.

"When Phoebe asks me to do her a favor, I will do it, but I think it's fair that she also returns a favor when I ask," explained Mark.

Phoebe looked at Mark, "When I ask you to help me out or do a favor for me, you remind me that I owe you. You keep track and then I feel obligated to do something nice right away, so you won't say, 'You owe me.'"

"Have you ever thought about just doing something nice for each other—without keeping score—because you love each other?" I asked.

"We tried that before," Phoebe spouted. "I was doing Mark's laundry and the grocery shopping, but he wasn't helping me with chores unless I asked him to help."

"Have you ever done favors for anyone outside of your relationship?" I asked with curiosity.

"I need to be appreciated," Mark spoke up. "If someone randomly does something nice for me, they appreciate me, and I feel obligated to return a favor as a way of thanking them."

"A simple 'thank you' when someone does you a favor won't do?" I asked. "Where did you learn 'give a favor; repay with a favor'?"

"My mom," Mark quickly replied. "If grandma sent me money for my birthday or friends gave me gifts, mom would say, 'Now make sure you return the favor, so they know you appreciate it.'"

"Did your mom raise you the same?" I questioned, looking at Phoebe.

"No. Mark taught me this when we started dating two years ago. It made sense at the time, but now I'm frustrated and it's annoying."

"If you really love someone, you will naturally want to do kind things for them," I said. "In fact, one of the qualities of love is kindness. If you are keeping track, are you doing favors out of obligation or love?"

They both stared at me without responding, so I continued. "If I do something kind for my husband because I love him, then I have no expectations for him to repay me. When he does kind things for me, I smile and say, 'Thank you honey.' If he expected me to repay the favor, it would seem obligatory, like there were strings attached and he was not doing it from his heart. He is not obligated to do me favors, nor do I feel obligated to do him favors. We are motivated to do kind things for each other because we love each other."

"I do love Mark," Phoebe blurted out. "But keeping track makes me feel obligated rather than spontaneously doing him a favor because I want to."

"Keeping track of favors comes from the mindset of 'you owe me now', which is self-centered rather than relationship-centered," I pointed out. "If you both decided to practice giving because you love each other, you would do kind favors when you wanted to without expecting a favor in return."

I asked both of them if they would be willing to practice loving each other every day without expectations, obligations, or tracking favors. I also invited them to ask themselves daily, "How can I let my partner know I love him/her without doing a favor?'

They agreed and came back to see me two weeks later.

Phoebe smiled as she sat down, "What a relief it has been to not keep track of favors. I'm not annoyed with Mark anymore. I let him know I love him by telling him and hugging him. I also cooked dinner for him twice and didn't expect a favor back."

I looked at Mark, "How do you think it went?"

He said, "It was hard. It seems like I shouldn't keep track of favors, but in my head I do."

"How did you let Phoebe know you love her without doing her a favor?" I asked.

"I told her, 'Thank you for being my girlfriend and being patient with me.' It feels weird to say these things rather than do her a favor," Mark floundered.

"If you want to do Phoebe a favor because you love her and it is coming from the kindness in your heart, then do it with no expectation for her to return it. I want you both to practice lovingly giving to each other to enhance the closeness in the relationship, not to get something in return. Remember relationship-centered giving, not self-centered getting."

"Got it," Mark nodded.

TIPS TO BECOME MORE RELATIONSHIP-CENTERED

- Compromise more instead of needing plans to go your way.
- Do not try to control your partner's opinions by getting angry when he/she doesn't agree with you.
- Ask your partner what he/she needs from you to have a good relationship with you.
- Make it easy for your partner to get along with you. Monitor your moods and practice having a positive attitude.
- Ask your partner how you can help if he/she is stressed.
- Share in household responsibilities and chores.

- If you need your partner to do something, ask politely rather than demanding.
- Support your partner in reaching his/her personal goals (health, career, finances, spiritual, self-esteem).
- Encourage your partner and let him/her know you are on his/her team.

Always be mindful of how your choices and behaviors affect your partner. Practice the Golden Rule:

> Do to others whatever you would like them to do to you.
>
> — Matthew 7:12 (NLT)

COUPLE'S JOURNAL

Answer the following questions, then discuss them as a couple.

1. Ask your partner if he/she thinks you are more self-centered or relationship-centered. Have him/her give you specific examples. Write this down.

_____

_____

_____

_____

_____

_____

_____

_____

_____

_____

_____

_____

_____

_____

2. What have you done to demonstrate you are relationship-centered to your partner? *(Example: I did not engage in an argument when I disagreed with my partner's opinion. I said uplifting words to my partner when he/she was having a discouraging day. I did my partner's laundry when he/she did not have time.)*

_____

_____

_____

_____

_____

_____

_____

_____

_____

_____

_____

3. What has your partner done to prove to you he/she is relationship centered? *(Example: He/She took my car to get fixed when I did not have the money. He/she supported me in a career change. He/she bought snore strips when I shared I could not sleep well because of his/her snoring.)*

_____

_____

_____

_____

_____

_____

_____

_____

_____

_____

_____

4. How can you be more relationship centered each day? *(Example: Be patient with my partner, ask my partner how I can make it easier for him/her to live with me, help my partner with more chores)*

Elisabeth Davies, M.C.

COUPLE'S HOMEWORK

Each day, ask yourself, "How can I enhance my relationship today?"

- Sunday:

- Monday:

- Tuesday:

- Wednesday:

- Thursday:

- Friday:

- Saturday:

If you cannot come up with an answer, ask your partner for suggestions; record them below.

_____

_____

_____

_____

_____

_____

Practice nurturing your partner and your relationship daily to strengthen your bond together.

LOVE TIP

Practice saying words in front of the mirror to yourself before saying them to your partner. This will help you become more aware of how your words may be received.

INTENTION

Before I decide, before I act,
I will think about how my words and behavior
will enhance our relationship in meaningful ways.

AFFIRMATION

I am a relationship-centered partner
because helping to meet [partner's name]'s needs
are just as important as mine.

Elisabeth Davies, M.C.

Chapter 17

Accepting Your Partner

Read this chapter together as a couple. Take time to discuss your thoughts and suggestions on becoming more accepting.

Accepting your partner means not trying to change him/her to be who you want him/her to be for you. This can be a challenge, but consistently practicing acceptance will help you avoid unnecessary disappointment and allow for deep connection. Being accepted by your partner allows you to express your real self and grow to your full potential as a person. If you or your partner do not fully accept each other, there are likely secrets between you that allow you to avoid rejection and protect yourself from judgment. Being accepted for who you are is one of the seven requirements for mental and emotional health.

REQUIREMENTS THAT DEVELOP EMOTIONAL HEALTH

- Being unconditionally loved.
- Being accepted for who you are.
- Feeling a sense of belonging to a person, group, or community.
- Feeling useful or competent.
- Being acknowledged and paid attention to.
- Feeling safe and secure.
- Feeling autonomous or in control over your environment.

Every human being has value and needs love and acceptance to be able to thrive mentally and emotionally.

Low self-esteem sabotages your ability to accept your partner, because if you do not accept yourself, you cannot accept your partner. In the same way, if you do not love yourself, you cannot fully love another. Self-criticism morphs into criticism of your partner.

Accepting your partner does not mean you agree with his/her choices, it means you are not the judge of his/her behavior or choices. You are not responsible or in control of anyone's behavior except your own. The more you practice loving and approving of your true self by forgiving your mistakes and being gentle with your imperfections, the more you will be able to extend this to your partner. And you will emotionally heal.

CLIENT STORY

Andrea wanted to heal her rigid views of her fiancé, Tye. They both came to me for help because they argued often and did not accept each other's choices. Neither of them would budge on who would conduct their marriage ceremony. Tye wanted a Catholic priest to marry them, and Andrea wanted her Baptist pastor to officiate.

Andrea explained, "I never cared what religion Tye was before we started planning our wedding. It was never an issue. But Tye's dad wants us to be married by the family priest, who married Tye's sister and brother, and my mom said she is not coming to our wedding if a Catholic priest officiates."

"Who is paying for the ceremony officiator?" I asked.

Tye said, "My dad said he will pay for our priest to do our wedding ceremony."

"I want my mom and dad to be at our wedding," Andrea loudly declared, glaring at Tye.

"If just both of you were to make the decision of who officiates your wedding without either of your parents getting in the middle of your wedding plans, who would you chose?" I asked. "Remember, you are both adults, and it is *your* wedding, not your parents."

Tye and Andrea looked at each other. Tye shrugged and Andrea said, "I really don't care who marries us as long as our marriage is legitimate."

"Can you afford to pay for your own priest or pastor?" I asked.

"We could call and get prices," Tye said, looking at Andrea.

I suggested Andrea tell her mother how important it is to her that she attend their wedding, but not allow her mom to be in control of selecting the person to officiate.

Andrea and Tye came back to see me three weeks later.

"Who did you decide to officiate your wedding?" I inquired.

Tye said, "Dad is going to pay for our family priest to officiate our wedding."

"How did it go talking with your mom?" I asked Andrea.

"Well, she's not happy about it. I can tell you that," Andrea laughed. "I took your advice and told her how important it is to me that she comes to my wedding. I explained my wedding is only a couple of hours. Can't you just please be there for me? We are still talking, so I think she's going to show up."

"Weddings can be stressful to plan." I said. "You have to remember you are both creating a life together and making decisions that help you build a strong, loving relationship with each other. Don't allow outside influences—whether it's your parents or someone else—to come between you or cause division in your marriage."

They both looked at each other and smiled. Andrea reached for Tye's hand. "It's you and me babe, forever. Mom will get over it, even if I'm marrying a Catholic!"

Accept one another, then, just as Christ has accepted you so that God will be given glory.

— Romans 15:7 (NLT)

TIPS FOR ACCEPTING YOUR PARTNER:

- Practice more self-acceptance so you can extend acceptance to your partner.
- Let go of your expectations of your partner. Ask what his/her expectations are of himself/herself. Keep these in mind when you become disappointed.
- Look for the good in your partner rather than focusing on what bothers you about him/her.
- Use kind words when asking your partner to do something for you, rather than demanding. He/she always has a right to say "yes" or "no" to your requests.
- Learn his/her habits and preferences and practice tolerance and flexibility rather than annoyance.
- Hold back from judging and criticizing. Set goals to not criticize yourself or your partner. You are not responsible for his/her words and behaviors.
- Ask God to help you love your partner as He does so you can be more forgiving of his/her imperfections.
- Take a mini break if you become intolerant of your partner's behavior. Go for a walk and breathe out all negativity. Come back when you can have a positive interaction.

- Ask your partner to give you feedback if you come across as judgmental so that you can behave more supportively.
- Do not take his/her words and behaviors personally. Everything your partner says is an expression of who he/she is in that moment. Focus on what is in your control (how you think, feel, or respond to each situation) so that you can respond in love.
- Your partner does not have to do things your way or take your advice. It is a partnership. Compromise and show flexibility and consideration to bolster harmony and connection with each other.

COUPLE'S JOURNAL

Answer the following questions individually, then share them with your partner.

1. How do you practice accepting yourself? *(Example: I forgive myself for my mistakes, I am gentle on myself when I do not do things I know I should, I recognize the good in myself)*

_____

_____

_____

_____

_____

_____

_____

_____

_____

_____

_____

_____

_____

_____

_____

Elisabeth Davies, M.C.

2. How do you show acceptance to your partner? *(Example: I do not criticize his/her political beliefs, I do not instigate arguments with my partner when he/she parents differently than I do, I do not say anything negative to my partner about his/her choices in friends and hobbies)*

_____

_____

_____

_____

_____

_____

_____

_____

_____

_____

_____

3. How does your partner show you he/she accepts you for who you are? *(Example: He/She lets me listen to the music I like even though he/she doesn't like it, he/she asks me to pick what I like when we go shopping, he/she encourages and supports me when I fail at personal goals)*

_____

_____

_____

_____

_____

_____

_____

_____

_____

_____

_____

4. Is/are there one or more qualities about your partner that is/are a struggle for you to accept? *(Example: He/She smokes or drinks too much, he/she has an anger problem, he/she is selfish)*

_____

_____

_____

_____

_____

_____

_____

_____

_____

_____

_____

_____

5. If you are doing something your partner does not like, how do you want him/her to respond to you? *(Example: Be curious about who I am and why I make the choices I do. Practice looking for the good in me, instead of focusing on my flaws. Practice more tolerance and gentleness toward me.)*

_____

_____

_____

_____

_____

_____

_____

_____

_____

_____

_____

_____

6. Ask your partner if they feel accepted by you. Ask for examples of ways that make him/her feel accepted by you. Record what your partner shares.

COUPLE'S HOMEWORK

Each day, practice accepting yourself and your partner by monitoring your thoughts, especially when they are critical.

Say to critical thoughts, "I choose to look for the positive in myself and my partner."

Pay attention to your words. If they are critical, apologize and say, "I don't mean to judge."

Hold yourself accountable to be more accepting so that you and your partner can become more emotionally healthy and reach your full potential.

Today, I was more accepting of my partner when I…

_____

_____

_____

_____

_____

_____

_____

_____

_____

_____

_____

_____

_____

_____

_____

_____

_____

_____

_____

_____

Elisabeth Davies, M.C.

LOVE TIP

Practice listening for the reasons your partner has the opinions and behaviors he/she maintains. Take time to hear what is important to him/her without judgment. This will help you both be more accepting of each other.

INTENTION

As I practice letting go of judging myself,
I allow more acceptance to flow in my relationship.

AFFIRMATION

I accept that [partner's name] and I
have different ideas, abilities, and values.
I honor these differences by letting go
of the need to change [partner's name].

Elisabeth Davies, M.C.

Chapter 18

Forgiving Your Partner

Read this chapter together as a couple. Take time to discuss your thoughts and suggestions on being more forgiving.

No one is perfect. Your partner and you will make mistakes and say and do things to each other that are hurtful and selfish. If either of you chooses not to forgive, bitterness and resentment will grow. The outcome will be an emotionally distant relationship, most likely riddled with arguments and compounded hurts.

Forgiveness does not mean forgetting. You will remember if your partner has wronged you. Forgiveness does not necessarily mean reconciling either. Forgiveness is internal. It happens in your heart and head. It does not require an apology from the person who wronged you. Forgiveness is a decision to release grudges or let go of wrongs committed against you. The result is freedom from the negative emotions caused by the wrong so that it becomes a neutral memory, absent of emotional pain. Forgiveness is necessary if you want a long-term relationship free of hurt.

It is natural to ask, "Is everything forgivable? How many times should I forgive the same mistake?"

In the Bible, Peter had these same questions:

> Then Peter came to him and asked, "Lord, how often should I forgive someone who sins against me? Seven times?"
>
> "No, not seven times," Jesus replied, "but seventy times seven!
>
> — Matthew 18:21-22 (NLT)

Wow! Is it humanly possible to forgive a person that many times?

Forgiveness is a spiritual quality, not a human one. Otherwise, we would all naturally, effortlessly forgive everyone who wrongs us, and there would be no human revenge or hate toward other people. Fortunately, forgiving is a choice and there are effective exercises that can help you hone this skill so that you can live a life free of long-standing hurt, bitterness, and resentment.

EXERCISES TO HELP YOU FORGIVE

1. Ask yourself, "How can I heal this hurt rather than have it continue to cause me pain?"

_____

_____

_____

_____

_____

_____

2. Ask yourself, "If I choose to forgive this wrong and no longer have any hurt or anger about it, how will it benefit me emotionally?"

_____

_____

_____

_____

_____

_____

_____

3. Ask yourself, "How is holding on to this wrong benefiting me emotionally?"

_____

_____

_____

_____

_____

_____

_____

Elisabeth Davies, M.C.

4. Talk to someone who has forgiven someone who wronged him/her. Ask how they forgave the wrong. Ask if there were any benefits to forgiving.

_____

_____

_____

_____

_____

_____

5. Practice looking at people through eyes of compassion. What could have prompted them to wrong you in the first place? What could be causing him/her so much hurt? People who carry unresolved emotional hurts project that hurt onto other people, continuing the cycle of hurt.

_____

_____

_____

_____

_____

_____

6. Think back on times you have been forgiven for your mistakes. How did this impact you?

_____

_____

_____

_____

_____

_____

CLIENT STORY

Gracie had an affair with her co-worker fifteen years into her marriage to Wendell.

Wendell told me during their first counseling session, "I feel hurt and betrayed. I cannot sleep because I am obsessing about Gracie's affair. I love her and want to be married to her. I just don't know how to forgive her."

"Gracie, what's going on?" I asked.

"I feel terrible about my affair with Terry. I never meant to hurt Wendell," she said apologetically.

"Is the affair still continuing?" I asked her.

"No, no, but I still work with Terry, and Wendell doesn't trust me when I'm at work. He wants me to quit my job."

"Do you want to continue being married to Wendell?" I asked.

"Of course, I do!" Gracie quickly blurted.

"If it was the other way around and Wendell had an affair with a co-worker, would you want him to continue working with her?" I inquired.

"No, I understand, but I have been at my job for almost seventeen years and I'm going to lose benefits, seniority…" she trailed off.

"Or, you could stay at your job and lose your marriage, if it's more important to you," I pointed out.

"If you're not willing to quit seeing Terry at work every week, then it's over!" Wendell angrily responded, looking at Gracie.

"Honey, I'm going to quit my job. Calm down. This is hard for me," Gracie's voice sounded strained.

"How am I going to forgive my wife?" Wendell asked, looking at me.

"I have a forgiveness exercise that I want you to practice each time you think about Gracie's affair," I suggested to Wendell. "When the thoughts come, I want you to respond by saying to them, 'I unconditionally forgive Gracie for having an affair with Terry.'"

"Just like that, I should forgive her? No consequence for cheating? I can't stop thinking about her affair!" Wendell was frustrated.

"Gracie gets natural consequences for her affair," I said, looking at Wendell. "Her infidelity caused your marriage to lose its foundation and stability. She now has a husband who no longer trusts her. A husband who has lost respect for her and now withholds love and intimacy. A husband who is distant and angry. And loss of her job and income if she wants to stay married to you. Gracie has a lot of work to do if she wants to continue having you as her husband."

Wendell was quiet, and so was Gracie.

I continued, "What consequence do you want Gracie to have for her affair?"

"I just wish it never happened," Wendell shook his head.

"Letting your mind and imagination run wild with thoughts of her affair rather than having a healing response to them is punishing to *you*, not Gracie," I commented.

"I will try the forgiveness exercise," Wendell promised.

"And you need to make a decision," I said, looking at Gracie. "Quit your job and save your marriage or stay at your job and lose your marriage."

Wendell and Gracie came back ten days later. Gracie said she had quit her job and was applying for a new one.

"How is the forgiveness exercise working, Wendell?" I asked.

"Terrific! I must have forgiven Gracie a hundred times a day, but I'm not angry at her anymore; I sleep better. I even let her back into our bed." He chuckled, looking at Gracie, who was smiling and reaching to hold his hand.

Wendell's decision to forgive Gracie and Gracie's decision to quit the affair and her job helped put their marriage back on course. I have counseled many couples who decided not to forgive an affair or terminate an affair and it wrecked their relationship.

Oftentimes, people choose not to forgive, consciously or subconsciously, as a way to protect themselves from future hurt from the person who wronged them. When you put walls of unforgiveness over your heart, you do not just block out the hurt, you also block out love, healing, and positive emotions from flowing through. Choosing to forgive is a gift you give to yourself.

Both you and your partner will say or do something at some point that needs to be forgiven. Forgiving your partner proves that you really love him/her. It also demonstrates that you possess spiritual qualities of extending grace and mercy.

COUPLE'S JOURNAL

Answer the following questions separately, then share them with your partner.

1. What are some things you have done that still cause feelings of regret? *(Example: Making poor choices, hurting someone, breaking promises)*

_____

_____

_____

_____

_____

_____

_____

2. What are some wrongs your partner committed that still cause you negative feelings? *(Example: He/She said hurtful words, he/she broke your trust, he/she made selfish choices)*

_____

_____

_____

_____

_____

_____

_____

3. Ask your partner if there are mistakes/wrongs he/she has not forgiven you for? *(Example: Lying, not making your relationship a priority, infidelity)*

_____

_____

_____

_____

_____

_____

_____

4. Ask your partner if there is anything you can do that would help him/her forgive. *(Example: Apologize, not repeat the same behavior, be more considerate of his/her feelings)*

_____

_____

_____

_____

_____

_____

_____

_____

_____

_____

5. Write down mistakes/wrongs you have forgiven your partner for.

_____

_____

_____

_____

_____

_____

_____

_____

_____

_____

_____

"To Forgive is to set a prisoner free and discover that the prisoner was you."
— Lewis Smedes

A GIFT TO YOUR PARTNER

Thank your partner for mistakes and wrongs they have forgiven you for. Share this with him/her.

1. Partner 1: Thank you for forgiving me for…

_____

_____

_____

_____

_____

_____

_____

_____

_____

_____

2. Partner 2: Thank you for forgiving me for…

_____

_____

_____

_____

_____

_____

_____

_____

_____

_____

_____

COUPLE'S HOMEWORK

If there are still memories that bring up hurt, anger, resentment, or bitterness when you recall them, you have not completely forgiven. Pick one unhealed memory at a time and practice this forgiveness exercise with it.

Recall the memory and say, "I unconditionally forgive [you or the person who wronged you] for doing or saying [wrong that was committed]."

_____

_____

_____

_____

_____

_____

_____

_____

_____

_____

_____

_____

_____

_____

_____

_____

_____

_____

_____

_____

_____

Practice this forgiveness exercise each time you recall old hurts until you no longer feel negative emotions (anger, bitterness, resentment, guilt, grudges).

LOVE TIP

Show more compassion to your partner when he/she makes mistakes.
Respond gently to his/her imperfections as you grow together in forgiveness.

INTENTION

I will practice forgiving myself
for all my hurtful words and behaviors
so that I can pass this grace on to my relationship.

AFFIRMATION

I forgive [partner's name]
so that I can be free of hurt
and grow in grace and mercy,
knowing this leads to more love
and emotional healing.

Elisabeth Davies, M.C.

Chapter 19

Reflecting on the Relationship You Are Creating

Answer the following questions separately, then share them with your partner.

Congratulations on completing this workbook! After much reflection and practice, you now know the skills necessary for a strong foundation and healthy relationship, as well as love tips to create intimacy, romance, adventure, and happiness together. Reflect on what you have learned about yourself, your partner, and the relationship you want to continuing creating together.

1. How have you grown as a partner? *(Example: I am more loving, respectful, and initiate adventure in my relationship)*

_____

_____

_____

_____

_____

_____

_____

_____

_____

_____

_____

_____

_____

_____

2. How has your partner grown? *(Example: He/She is more trustworthy, he/she is more affectionate, he/she is more committed to the relationship)*

_____

_____

_____

_____

_____

_____

_____

_____

_____

_____

_____

_____

_____

_____

_____

_____

_____

_____

_____

_____

_____

_____

_____

_____

_____

_____

_____

_____

_____

_____

3. What are you working on to create a better future together? *(Example: We are practicing being more accepting of each other, we are becoming more relationship centered in our decision-making, we are encouraging each other in personal growth)*

_____

_____

_____

_____

_____

_____

_____

_____

_____

_____

_____

_____

_____

_____

_____

_____

_____

_____

_____

_____

_____

_____

_____

4. What thoughts, ideas, goals, or plans do you have for the amazing relationship you and your partner are building?

Endnotes

i   Framingham, Jane. "How Our Social Network Helps Us Thrive." Psych Central, January 14, 2020. https://psychcentral.com/lib/how-our-social-network-helps-us-thrive/.

ii   Pelley, Virginia. "The Divorce Rate is Different Than You Think." Fatherly, November 11, 2020. https://www.fatherly.com/love-money/what-is-divorce-rate-america/.

iii   Thompson, Dennis. "Americans Still Making Unhealthy Choices: CDC." WebMD (WebMD), May 21, 2013. https://www.webmd.com/a-to-z-guides/news/20130521/americans-still-making-unhealthy-choices-cdc.

iv   Today Show. "Falling in Love? Here's How Long the Passion Will Last." TODAY.com, February 14, 2019. https://www.today.com/health/how-long-does-passion-last-four-stages-love-t108471.

v   Hansen-Bundy, Benjy. "What Men Get Wrong About Sex, According to a Relationship Therapist." GQ, February 2014. https://www.gq.com/story/esther-perel-what-men-get-wrong-about-sex

vi   "Happiness Research: What Makes You Happy?" @berkleywellness, November 2015. https://www.berkeleywellness.com/healthy-mind/mind-body/article/what-science-happiness

vii   "Tagged as Pessimism." Wellness, February 2020. https://www.wellness.com/documents/tag/pessimism

About the Author

Elisabeth Davies, M.C., holds a master's degree in counseling and has been a counselor since 1989. In 2005, she founded Good Things Emotional Healing, LLC and is author of the *Good Things Emotional Healing* workbooks and affirmation cards. Elisabeth has been happily married to her husband since 1993. They have two adult children and two grandchildren. Visit her website at **www.ElisabethDavies. com** or follow her on Instagram @elisabeth.davies.

ABOUT THE ILLUSTRATOR

Bryan R. Marshall is an artist and illustrator based in Vancouver, Canada. Bryan works in both digital and traditional media and has been freelancing in graphic design and illustration for over two decades. Visit his website at **BryanRMarshall.com** or follow him on Instagram @bryan.r.marshall.

OTHER BOOKS BY THIS AUTHOR AND ILLUSTRATOR

- *Good Things Emotional Healing Journal: Addiction*

CPSIA information can be obtained
at www.ICGtesting.com
Printed in the USA
LVHW111652250122
709359LV00013B/311